OUR HERITAGE:

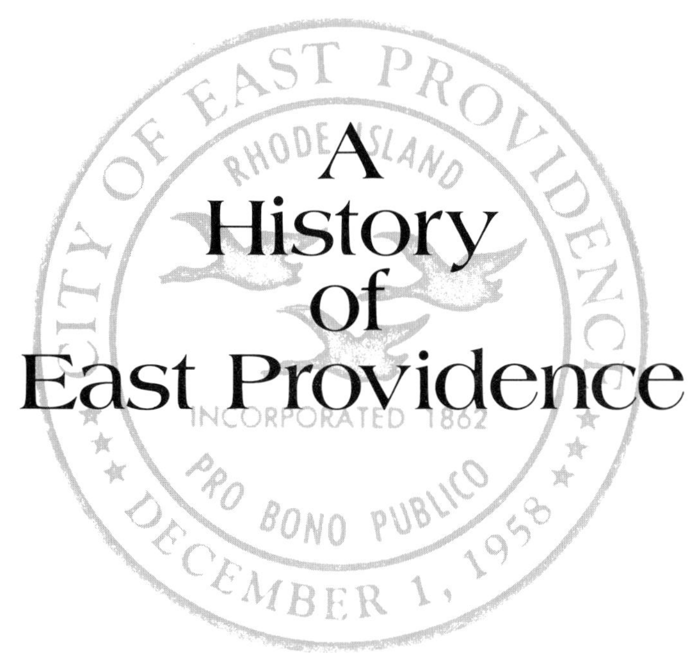

A History of East Providence

Monarch Publishing, Inc.
White Plains · New York

Researched and written by
Joseph Conforti
Staff Writer
Monarch Publishing, Inc.

Photographic credits

Mr. Dennis Mullervy – slides
Mr. Doug Gamage – photographs
Mr. and Mrs. George Chalko – post cards
Mr. Harold Flint – map

14 Mamaroneck Avenue
White Plains, New York 10601
Printed in the United States of America

Library of Congress Catalog Card Number: 75-27782

AUTHOR'S ACKNOWLEDGMENTS

A number of East Providence residents aided me in the preparation of this history. Professor Robert Deasy of Providence College gave generously of his time and helped me in many ways—from locating written sources to introducing me to many of the people whose names appear below. Dennis Mullervy, President of the East Providence Historical Society, was equally helpful in supplying me with material and offering suggestions while I was researching and writing the history. Harold Flint of Riverside allowed me the use of unpublished and published material relating to the history of East Providence that he and his father had accumulated over the years.

Of others who helped me I would like particularly to thank: Len Erickson of Rumford; James Beeley, East Providence City Clerk; David Howard, Editor of the *East Providence Post;* Edwin Pritchard, Charlotte Phillips Pritchard and Michael McNamara of the Washburn Wire Company; Dr. Karl Holst of the Rumford Chemical Works; Richard Longstreth of the Rhode Island State Historical Preservation Commission; Lt. Norman Gladding of the East Providence Fire Department; Godfrey Allen of Narragansett Terrace; Charles Gravlin of Phillipsdale; Stephen Walsh of Rumford; Virginia DaMota of the East Providence School System; and Owen Reid of Providence.

Finally, George Thompson, Charles O'Connell, Katherine Rodman and Eugene A. Amaral of the East Providence Bicentennial Committee read an early draft of the history and made a number of valuable suggestions which improved the manuscript.

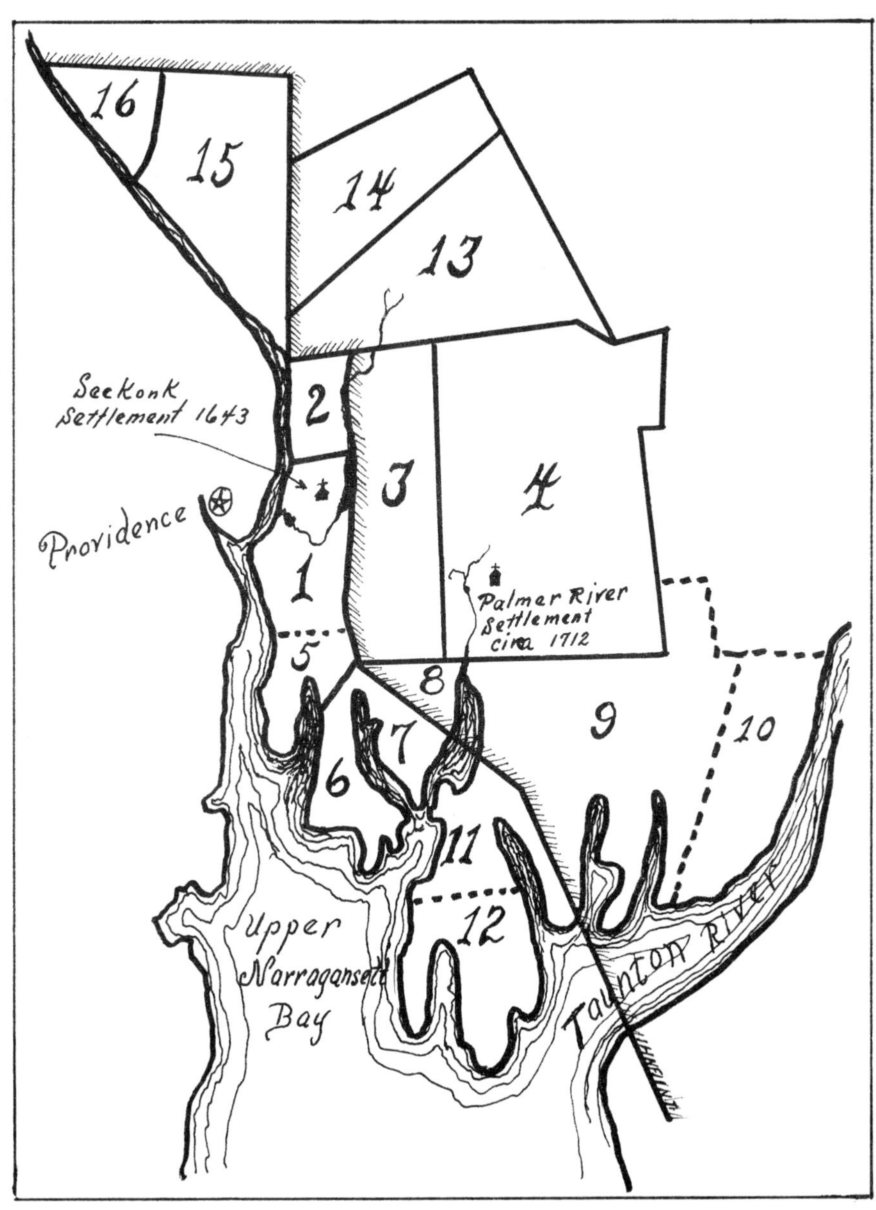

Map of purchases prepared by Mr. Harold Flint

KEY TO MAP

Areas 1, 2, 3 and 4 made up the town of Seekonk in 1643. In 1645 the name of the town was changed from Seekonk to Rehoboth at the request of the settlers.

Area 4 was the first section to break away from the mother town in 1812. The town was split in half with the new town, the eastern part, keeping the name of Rehoboth while the old part of the town, the western section, once again took its original name, Seekonk. Settlement of the eastern portion of the town began in the early 1700s.

Area 3: The town was again split in two with the changing of the Rhode Island and Massachusetts boundary line in 1862, the eastern half of the town going to Massachusetts and the western half going to the state of Rhode Island. The eastern half of the town retained the name of Seekonk, thereby taking both names that had been associated with the history of the mother town.

Area 2: This section of what was left of the old town of Seekonk became a part of Pawtucket, Rhode Island, in 1862.

Area 1: In 1862, the oldest inhabited part of the original town, along with a part of old Wannamoisett (Riverside) became East Providence and was also joined to Rhode Island, leaving Seekonk without church or industry. It also brought to Rhode Island a history predating its own.

Areas 5, 6, 7 and 8 were Wannamoisett, now Riverside, Barrington, and a small portion of Swansea. This purchase was made by John Brown in 1645.

Areas 9, 10, and 11 belonged to Swansea when it was founded in 1668, and Wannamoisett left the town of Rehoboth to also become a part of Swansea.

Areas 6, 7 and 8 became Barrington in 1717, with 5, Riverside, added.

Areas 11, Warren, and 12, Bristol, along with 6 and 7, Barrington, became a part of Rhode Island in 1747. Areas 6 and 7 were joined to 11 and became Warren. Area 5, Riverside, then went back to Rehoboth 1, 2, 3, and 4.

Area 12 fell to Plymouth Colony by right of conquest after King Philip's war, and was incorporated in 1681. Bristol came to Rhode Island with the changing of the boundary in 1747. In 1770 Barrington, 6 and 7, split from Warren, 11, and remains the same today. Somerset, 10, split from Swansea in 1790, leaving Swansea with areas 8 and 9.

Areas 13, 14, 15 and 16 were the Rehoboth North Purchase of 1661.

Area 13 became Attleboro in 1694.

Area 14 broke from Attleboro in 1887 to become North Attleboro.

Area 15 broke away from Attleboro in 1747 to become Cumberland.

Area 16 broke away from Cumberland in 1867 to become Woonsocket.

All of the above-mentioned towns were at one time a part of the old town of Rehoboth (areas 1, 2, 3 and 4) or under its protectorate.

ACKNOWLEDGMENTS

The East Providence Bicentennial Committee acknowledges the unfailing support of the City Council of 1973 which appointed it: Mayor Martin P. Slepkow, Anthony A. Almeida, Mary Lou Blecharzyck, James W. Driscoll, William A. Wilson; and the 1975 City Council: Mayor George A. Lamb, Anthony A. Almeida, Edward J. Doyle, James W. Driscoll and William A. Wilson. Their continued enthusiasm for the programs and activities of the Committee has been invaluable. Our citizens can be proud of the position taken by the Council. Their support has been exceptional, and outstanding among the cities of the State. City Manager Paul A. Flynn and all City Departments have given willing cooperation.

Energetic activity of the Ways and Means Subcommittee and the cooperation of many citizens have given welcome financial support.

TABLE OF CONTENTS

Prologue:
From Old Rehoboth to Old Seekonk to East Providence

In 1862, when East Providence was incorporated as a part of Rhode Island, many older residents of the community could proudly boast of having lived in three towns and two states without ever having moved. Shifting geographical boundaries and political jurisdictions make up a good part of the history of the territory which since 1862 has been called East Providence. Because the history of East Providence winds its way through three towns and counties and two states, it is important for the reader to have at the outset a clear overview of these important geographical and political changes.

In 1641 the Plymouth Colony purchased from the Indians a large tract of land which today includes the northern half of East Providence (from Watchemoket to Rumford), Rehoboth, Seekonk and part of Pawtucket. Four years later, John Brown of Plymouth bought a considerably smaller piece of land from the Indians which today comprises the southern half of East Providence (Riverside), Barrington and a small part of Swansea. Finally, in 1661, Plymouth completed the "North Purchase" from which Attleboro, North Attleboro and Cumberland were later formed. These three purchases brought under the control of white authorities a huge tract of land heavily wooded and hilly in some places, flat and clear in others, surrounded by natural waterways, blessed with clear inland streams and brooks, and plagued by the rocky terrain which tested the endurance of even the most hearty pioneer farmer of New England. Over the whole the authorities gave the name

'Rehoboth,' and in the course of more than two centuries the communities named above were carved from the original settlement.

The center of this large settlement, which is sometimes referred to as 'Old Rehoboth,' is to be found within the borders of modern East Providence. Shifting boundary lines carried the locations of Old Rehoboth's first meeting-house, home lots, town green and common pasture land – in short, the heart of Old Rehoboth – to East Providence. But the journey was not direct; the jurisdiction of Old Seekonk intervened between the claims of Old Rehoboth and the incorporation of East Providence. In 1812 the western half of Old Rehoboth was set off as a separate township called Seekonk, Massachusetts. Old Rehoboth's town center now became the bustling heart of old Seekonk. Finally, in 1862 the western part of Old Seekonk was ceded to Rhode Island and incorporated as East Providence. "New" Seekonk repeated the experience of "New" Rehoboth fifty years earlier. In each case a good portion of the communities' population and a majority of their churches, schools, businesses and good roads came under the authority of a new town.

Needless to say, the subjects of these changes – the people first in Rehoboth, and then in Seekonk, who did not live within the new territorial boundaries and whose communities were drained of their lifeblood – were deeply upset by the course of events. Indeed, in 1862 the remaining inhabitants of Seekonk were so incensed by the establishment of East Providence that they pulled up and destroyed newly placed markers identifying the boundary line between the two towns.

In one sense, then, the history of East Providence overlaps with the history of other nearby towns, most notably Rehoboth and Seekonk. But looked at another way – in light of the fact that modern East Providence contains not only the territory which embraced the center of Old Rehoboth and Old Seekonk but also most of their historical remnants (original buildings, graveyards, historic sites and descendants) – one could conclude that not simply more territory became a part of Rhode Island in 1862 but more history as well. For this reason, the terms 'Old Rehoboth' and 'Old Seekonk' will be used to distinguish those historic communities, of which Rumford in present day East Providence was the center, from the modern towns of Rehoboth and Seekonk.

I
Settlement in the Wilderness

The territory which in 1862 became the Town of East Providence was in the mainstream of early American history. The original settlement and development of the area take us back to two of the most famous movements in our history—the coming of the Pilgrims to Plymouth and the Puritans to the Boston area. Both groups contributed settlers, ideas and disagreements to the early history of Old Rehoboth; therefore, it is important to look briefly at these deeply religious founders of New England.

The Pilgrims and Puritans were dissenting offshoots of the Church of England. Where the Pilgrims wanted to separate completely from England's "corrupt" established church, the Puritans wished simply to reform or purify it. In the new world each looked upon the other with suspicion. A small group of Pilgrims (101) landed in Plymouth in 1620 after twelve years of living in Holland. Ten years later, a larger (about 1,000), better financed and organized group of Puritans landed in Boston. Shortly after the establishment of both Plymouth and Massachusetts Bay colonies a familiar story began. Settlers started pushing out into the virgin wilderness, acquiring land from the Indians, clearing away the underbrush, building houses and barns and gradually developing communities which eventually would be recognized as new towns. So the history of Old Rehoboth begins, with most of the first inhabitants coming from Massachusetts Bay and political control and legal authority flowing from Plymouth.

The first white settler of Old Rehoboth was William Blackstone, a migrant from Massachusetts Bay. Blackstone had come to America in 1625, settled in the Boston area, and was well established by the time the Puritans arrived in 1630. Shortly after the invasion of his countrymen, Blackstone decided to seek a more peaceful retreat in the New England wilderness. He sold most of his land to Massachusetts Bay authorities in 1634, and a year later he settled in what is now Cumberland, Rhode Island, on the banks of the river which bears his name. Blackstone thus became the first white settler of Rhode Island, although during his lifetime his extensive property remained within the jurisdiction of Plymouth Colony.

Blackstone's journey from the Boston area was retraced a year later by a man who was to become his close friend and a heroic figure in American history. In 1636 Roger Williams began his exile from Massachusetts. Williams' stormy career among the Puritans started immediately upon his arrival from England in 1631. He had been invited to preach to the Boston Church in the place of its minister who was temporarily returning to England. Once in America Williams refused the offer because the congregation had not separated from the Church of England. When the Boston Puritans learned that members of the Salem Church wanted Williams to become their minister, the authorities warned Salem of his radical views, and as a result, Williams turned to Plymouth where his belief in "separatism" was more compatible with the ideas of the Pilgrims.

But Plymouth officials were not especially sympathetic to Williams, for in addition to encouraging churches to separate from the Church of England he denied civil authorities the right to compel church attendance, to enforce the first four commandments, and to claim lands acquired from the Indians. Neither Massachusetts Bay nor Plymouth could tolerate such radical challenges to their authority and it was only a matter of time before Williams was banished for good.

The end began in 1634 when the members of the Salem Church again decided to ask the strong-minded Puritan to become their pastor. The political and religious leaders of Boston, however, refused to stand by idly and allow their neighbors to ordain Williams and thereby establish heresy in their midst. In Massachusetts the government worked hand in hand with the church to insure religious orthodoxy and compel church attendance. The political leaders were referred to as "nursing fathers of the church," always careful to preserve its interests.

The Roger Williams plaque was placed on this oak tree in 1936, during Rhode Island's Tercentennial celebration.

Thus as an arm of the church, the government in Boston attempted to reverse the decision of the Salem Puritans to ordain Williams. The General Court of Massachusetts used the Salem Church's petition for a land grant as a bargaining device. The success of the petition, the government pointed out, depended upon the dismissal of Williams. Outraged by this action, Williams raised his attacks on civil authority to new heights. He protested that the charter establishing Massachusetts was not legitimate, and that the Colony's land still belonged to the Indians. He maintained that a person who had experienced religious conversion should not pray with one who had not, even if this person was his wife or child. Finally, he demanded that his church withdraw from contact with all the other "impure" churches of Massachusetts.

Williams lost much of the support within his church and had nearly all of the civil and religious leaders arrayed against him. He was summoned to appear before the General Court in October of 1635, where he refused to retract any of his statements. He was then ordered to leave the colony within six weeks, although this was later extended to the following spring. In the meantime, however, the government learned that "he had drawn about twenty persons to his opinion, and they

Roger Williams' spring and its plaque (below), located off Roger Williams Avenue in East Providence, marked the first settlement by the religious leader and his followers in their flight from Plymouth Colony. They would find a permanent haven in Providence in 1636, while the area of their first settlement became part of Rhode Island in 1862. A new granite marker was dedicated by the Bicentennial Committee in November of 1975.

were intended to erect a plantation about the Narragansett Bay, from whence the infection would easily spread into these churches. . ." To prevent Williams' escape the government decided to arrest him and ship him back to England. Williams managed to elude his captors and to begin his trek from Massachusetts in January of 1636.

By early spring he and his small band of followers were ready to begin their settlement. They chose a site near Seekonk Cove (now Omega Pond), at Roger Williams spring off Roger Williams Avenue in present day East Providence, and purchased the land from the Indians. The settlement and area around it was called Seekonk, the Indian term for the numerous black geese who found a natural habitat in the cove nearby.

The settlers began to build houses and to sow spring crops, all the while assuming that they were in Narragansett country. But in the summer of 1636, Williams was informed by Governor Edward Winslow of Plymouth that he was still within the confines of territory claimed by the Pilgrim colony. Thus began what would become a two hundred twenty-six year long boundary dispute between Rhode Island and Massachusetts which would not be finally settled until East Providence was incorporated in 1862.

In early summer Williams and his small band of followers collected their belongings, left their crops to be harvested by the Indians, boarded canoes and headed across the river to found Providence. In 1636, then, on land purchased from the Indians, the settlement called Providence was born, and it received a charter from the government in England in 1644.

In the meantime, back across the Seekonk River, other settlers began to occupy the land that Williams was forced to abandon. With Williams' help and encouragement a group of Charlestown residents launched another settlement at Seekonk Cove in 1638. By 1640, however, most of these Puritan pioneers had joined the colony of Providence, and the few who remained behind would soon join the first permanent settlement of "the land of the black geese."

In 1641, for the meager sum of two pounds and ten shillings, Governor Winslow of Plymouth and John Brown, one of his assistants, purchased from Massasoit, chief of the Wampanoag Indians, an "eight mile square" tract of land, which today includes East Providence, Seekonk, Rehoboth and part of Pawtucket. The preliminaries to settling the township (granting home lots, clearing the land, and erecting houses) now began and, probably in 1645, the Reverend Samuel Newman of Weymouth led the first wave of Puritans to the recently acquired land. Newman was born, educated and ordained in England, and, along with a large number of his fellow Puritans, he left his homeland in 1636 when persecutions by Church of England authorities were rapidly increasing. A learned man who had graduated with honors from Oxford and who was deeply involved in writing Biblical works, Newman settled first in Boston and then, in 1639, became the minister of the church at Weymouth.

The Newman colony numbered fifty-eight heads of households, and when women, children and other dependents are added, their total climbed to well over two hundred. Although a sprinkling of Pilgrims from towns (Taunton and Plymouth most notably) in Plymouth Colony were included among the original settlers, by and large Newman's colony consisted of Puritan migrants from Weymouth, Braintree and Hingham in Massachusetts Bay. Undoubtedly these pioneers of the East Providence area looked to their minister not only for spiritual guidance but for advice on the day to day problems which arose in forming a new township. Indeed, the lives of the people of early New England revolved around their fields and their churches.

The Newman plaque, erected at the cemetery across from the church in 1929, marks the first permanent settlement of the area called Rehoboth by the Puritan minister, Rev. Samuel Newman, and his followers.

The Phanuel Bishop house, built in 1771, is on the site of the original Newman parsonage on the "Ring of the Green" in Old Rehoboth.

The layout of the Seekonk settlement underlined the importance of agriculture and religion in the New England town. The first church, called a meeting-house because it was used for all public gatherings and not only for religious services, was begun in 1646 and completed in 1648. It was most likely a small, one-room, barn-like structure rather than the fabled, steepled white church (present day Newman Congregational Church in Rumford, for example) of later New England fame. In spite of its crude appearance, the meeting-house was at the center of the town with houses and fields radiating out from it. All of the inhabitants of the town were obliged to contribute to Rev. Newman's salary, to provide him with food and to supply him with firewood. Thus the respected minister, probably the only one with a college education in the new settlement, was freed from some of his daily burdens to devote more of his time to the work of the Lord. Newman, however, like nearly all ministers was also a farmer. Between reading the Bible, preparing sermons and writing theological works, he cultivated the soil which the town had given him with his parsonage (now the site of the Phanuel Bishop house).

After comfortably establishing the minister in his parsonage, the town proceeded to provide for the next most important individual in the settlement—the schoolmaster. Both the Puritans and Pilgrims who settled in Seekonk placed a high value on education. In the first place, children had to be taught how to read so that they could study the Bible. Secondly, because children were born evil, corrupt, and guilty of original sin, only religious conversion could save them. It was crucial, therefore, that they be taught the doctrines of the Calvinist faith in order to prepare for future conversion.

Recognizing the value of education as a bulwark to their religion, the Puritans established strict school laws. In 1647, for example, Massachusetts Bay passed its historic school act which is credited with introducing the concept of public education in America. The law stipulated that when towns had grown to include fifty households, local authorities had to appoint a schoolmaster "to teach all such children as shall resort to him to write and read. . ." The schoolmaster's salary was to be "paid either by the parents or masters of such children, or by the inhabitants in general. . ."

Old Rehoboth and other towns in Massachusetts Bay and Plymouth colonies may have established the forerunners of modern local public school systems. But the teaching methods in Calvinist New England were far from modern or democratic. Since children were evil, discipline was appropriately severe. Both parents and schoolmasters freely used a birch rod to punish children because, as one Puritan minister advised, "it will break neither bone nor skin. . .but it would break the bond that bindeth up corruption in the heart." "Better whipped than damned," wrote the famous Cotton Mather in summarizing the child rearing and educational views of seventeenth century New England.

Education in Old Rehoboth, then, was highly moralistic and stressed the guilt and evilness of the child. The *New England Primer,* a reading text which was most likely used in the town, introduced a student to the alphabet with such statements as "in Adam's fall, we sinned all." Memorization and rote-learning larded with heavy doses of discipline, rather than originality and open expression, became the characteristics of instruction.

Old Rehoboth set aside a home lot for its schoolmaster, and the townspeople paid his salary, usually in products (wheat, corn, firewood, etc.), not in money. The town's early schoolmasters are not identified in the records, but Reverend Newman probably filled the position in the early years and, later, college students or graduates studying to become ministers were hired. These schoolmasters seldom stayed in the town for more than a year.

All property in the town, including the home-lots of the minister and teacher, joined at a large "Ring of the Green"—an open "common" field at the center of the settlement. Each homeowner was obliged to erect a "common fence" in front of his property so that the "Ring of the Green" was entirely enclosed. Tradition has it, that the land hungry settlers would from time to time edge their "common fence" forward, and thereby enlarge their private property at the expense of the town green.

Behind the houses which fronted on the "Ring of the Green" lay the fields belonging to each homestead. The site of this town ring is in present day Rumford, within the area bounded by Greenwood Avenue, Elm Street, Bourne, Hoyt, Pawtucket and Bishop Avenues and Pleasant Street. Land within the "Ring of the Green" was set aside as a common pasture. The inhabitants' cows were kept here and tended by an Indian named Sam who was later given full rights within the settlement. In addition to house lots, farm lots, and common pasture, the town set aside

The modern Rumford sign, erected by the Rumford Women's Garden Club in 1951, marks the area that was once the common pasture land of the colonial settlement.

wood lots where the inhabitants could gather the tremendous supply of wood they used in their fireplaces for heating and cooking. The remaining land within the settlement was held by the town in common and was distributed over the years by drawing lots.

A few dirt roads crossed the town green, connecting one end of the village with another. All of the inhabitants were obliged to devote at least four days of work every year to the upkeep or laying out of roads. In front of the meeting-house stood the stocks and whipping post, ready to be used against any resident who did not fulfill his obligations concerning highway work, tax payments, church attendance or other matters.

If the meeting-house was austere in appearance, the houses which clustered around it were equally grim in the early years. The actual settlement of the township had to be delayed until homes were constructed. Since a saw mill was not immediately built, boards had to be carried to Seekonk from other towns. For some people logs, thatched roofs and earth floors provided protection from the elements. Many of these first homes, whether constructed of logs or boards, were small and only temporary shelters.

Gradually larger, more comfortable homes were erected and the old structures were converted to barns or outhouses. Clapboards, shingles and planks replaced log walls, thatched roofs and earth floors. Heavy frames of oak made these new houses sturdy structures. Windows remained few and small because of the problem of heating in the bitter winters. Glass was not readily available in the first years of settlement, so people used cloth and oiled paper in their windows. These homes remained relatively small, consisting of two or three rooms with, in many cases, a lean-to bedroom or kitchen in the back and a loft for storage. A large fireplace in the center of the house was constantly in use for cooking and heating. As the seventeenth century wore on houses grew larger and began to be erected in two stories. Roomy garrison houses where inhabitants huddled when Indians were on the warpath were built in different parts of the settlement. The most famous of these, the Noah Newman garrison house, was constructed in 1668 on the Town Green and was probably the largest and most beautiful house in the settlement. It most likely had a fireplace in each room. More important, it saved the residents of the town from the rampaging Indians during King Philip's War.

Most houses in the settlement remained small and even if they were improvements over the early shelters, they continued to be rather drab and plain, with low ceilings and dark interiors broken only by a little sunlight during the day and burning candles at night. Moreover, on the average a woman would give birth to seven or eight children. Captain Thomas Willett of Wannamoisett, for example, fathered thirteen children, a number that was fairly common in the seventeenth century. Contrary to what is widely believed, a high percentage of children and mothers survived the experience of childbirth. Thus such relatively large families made the typical home a rather crowded place in which to live.

The early settlers lived under convenants, that is, mutual agreements. First, New Englanders had a covenant with God, who had selected them as His "chosen people" to build a holy land in America. Next the residents of the Seekonk settlement formed a covenant with one another to try to live in harmony, cooperation and obedience under town authorities, and in this way to further God's grand design for New England. The inhabitants formed the first town government and signed the following covenant in 1644:

> *We whose names are underwritten, being by the Providence of God inhabitants of Seekonk, intending there to settle, do covenant and bind ourselves one to another, to subject our persons (and our property) to nine persons, . . .and we do (pledge ourselves) to be subject to all the wholesome (laws and orders made) by them, and to assist them, according to our ability and estate, and to give timely notice unto them of any such thing as in our conscience may prove dangerous unto the plantation. .*

The nine chosen townsmen fulfilled the function of the modern town council and met every forty days to handle the business of the settlement. The following townsmen elected in 1644 were the first officials of the settlement: Alexander Winchester, Richard Wright, Henry Smith, Edward Smith, Walter Palmer, William Smith, Stephen Payne, Richard Bowen and Robert Martin.

The earliest years of the town's history witnessed serious violations of the cooperative pledge contained in Seekonk's covenant. Nothing less than a full-fledged struggle for control of the town's government followed settlement. Since most of the inhabitants of Seekonk came from Massachusetts Bay, officials in that colony believed that they held authority over the new settlement. But the minority of residents from Plymouth and officials of that colony contended that the settlement was within territory granted to the Pilgrims, and Seekonk rightfully belonged to Plymouth Colony. Finally, in September of 1644 the Commissioners of the United Colonies of New England (representatives of all the colonies in the region) settled the dispute by awarding Seekonk to Plymouth. But the settlers from Massachusetts Bay did not give up without a fight. The town records of December 1644, for example, refer to "many meetings" and "great trouble" which stemmed from "controversies between party and party." The following year, 1645, was a turning point for the township. Its name was changed, the settlement was incorporated, new leadership took over the government, more land was added and orderly development began.

On June 4, 1645 the Plymouth General Court voted "That Seacunke be called Rehoboth." This change was requested by the inhabitants of the town and the source of the new name is generally considered to be the Reverend Samuel Newman. Upon settling in the area, Newman proclaimed to his people that "The Lord hath made room for us," and suggested that Rehoboth, a Biblical term meaning wide or open space, was an appropriate name for the new settlement. Once the jurisdictional dispute between Plymouth and Massachusetts Bay was resolved, the Seekonk settlement was incorporated as the town of Rehoboth.

At this time Plymouth people gradually began to assume control of town affairs and offices, replacing Massachusetts men. In the aftermath of this change, some disgruntled settlers even returned to Weymouth and Hingham. Samuel Newman continued as the town's minister, but his influence, like the influence of most Old Rehoboth inhabitants from Massachusetts, was considerably lessened. The new power in Old Rehoboth was John Brown (unrelated to the famous Brown family of Providence) who was an assistant (appointed representative) in the General Court of Plymouth and who had, along with Governor Winslow, made the original purchase of land for the town from the Indians.

On the basis of his political position, Brown was the leader of the Plymouth group which had joined the residents of Weymouth, Braintree and Hingham in settling Seekonk. When Plymouth established its jurisdiction over the town, Brown became the dominant political force in the community. Brown and his wife, daughter and two sons had come from England in 1632 and settled at Plymouth. In 1638 Brown joined with perhaps the most famous military man of early New England, Captain Myles Standish, in settling Taunton. When in 1643 the Board of Commissioners of the United Colonies of New England, which ruled in the dispute between Plymouth and Massachusetts over Seekonk, was established, Brown became one of its select members. Finally, in 1645 he was chosen chairman of Old Rehoboth's townsmen or town council.

Clearly, Brown was one of the most important men in all New England and easily the major figure in the early history of Old Rehoboth. His powerful voice was heard in three communities: as an assistant in Plymouth, a social leader in Taunton, and an official political leader in Rehoboth. Thus Brown conveniently maintained his residence at Taunton until 1655, so that he could easily survey and be equidistant from the other points–Old Rehoboth to the west and Plymouth to the east–in his political empire.

In addition to the name change and the rise to power of John Brown, 1645 also saw the second large purchase of land from the Indians. Massasoit offered to sell the town a tract of land which the Indians called Wannamoisett, meaning "at a good fishing place." The records of the town for December 29, 1645 spell out the terms of the purchase:

> *"Whereas there was a second agreement made with the Indians for their full consent in their removing from Wannamoisett and the value of fifteen pounds sterling to be paid them, or thereabouts in several commodities: it was in several town meetings expounded that if any one man would pay the particular purchase, they should have that land, with twelve acres lying at Watchemoket Cove, and so much more land at Wannamoisett as should be thought worth the payment of the same."*

Thus for only fifteen pounds any one could have bought the area which today comprises Riverside, Barrington and a small part of Swansea. In 1645, and indeed for a long time after, the area was not simply "a good fishing place," but probably one of the best fishing places in New England. Shellfish were in particularly abundant supply, as the representatives of the town discovered when they surveyed the territory and saw shells of all shapes and kinds along the sandy shore, giving evidence that the Indians had been feasting on the treasures of the sea for years. Indeed, Wannamoisett was for the Indians what it would later become to Rhode Islanders and New Englanders in general–a summer watering hole with excellent beaches and seafood. Each summer the Wampanoags camped along Narragansett Bay in Wannamoisett to be cooled by ocean breezes and to indulge themselves with the mouth-watering delicacies which they found around them.

In 1645 the already mighty John Brown bought Wannamoisett for fifteen pounds and further enhanced his wealth in land and his social and political standing. When in 1655, at the age of seventy-six, Brown retired from politics and deeded his Taunton homestead to relatives, he moved to Wannamoisett to live with his son, James, who had established his household on the land his father had purchased. From 1645 to 1667 Wannamoisett was a part of Old Rehoboth. When Old Swansea (really present day Swansea, Barrington, Warren and Somerset) was incorporated in 1667, Wannamoisett came under the jurisdiction of that town. Finally, in 1746, much of the area reverted to Old Rehoboth and was destined to become, in the following century, the fashionable resort area of Riverside.

With the purchase of Wannamoisett and the resolution of political control in 1645, the future of the settlement appeared to be bright. But religious controversies persisted for a number of years, which demonstrates how civil and religious authority were intertwined in the New England town. In 1649 nine members of Samuel Newman's church, who had disagreed with their minister's teachings for several years, withdrew from his congregation to form a Baptist church of their own. The dissenters were led by Obadiah Holmes, a native of England who had come to Massachusetts in 1639, had been excommunicated from the church in Salem shortly thereafter and had journeyed to Old Rehoboth in 1646. In 1649 he was chosen minister of the Baptist defectors.

Rev. Newman could not passively accept such a challenge to his authority and dangerous threat to the orderly religious life of the town. Aggravating Newman's uneasiness was the reality, as one historian has described it, of Old Rehoboth's "proximity to Providence and its plantations, where there was a universal toleration, the practice of free inquiry was encouraged, and principle, fancy, whim and conscience, all conspired to lessen the veneration of ecclesiastical authority." Indeed, as Roger Williams reported to Governor Winthrop of Massachusetts, the area appeared to be fast becoming a hotbed of Baptist dissent as the "way of new baptism spreads at Seekonk as well as Providence and the Island (Newport)."

Newman, then, marshaled all the power at his command to immunize Old Rehoboth against the Baptist contagion. First the minister excommunicated the dissenting parishioners. Next he aroused civil authorities to action. Petitions from Old Rehoboth, Taunton, the ministers of Plymouth Colony and the government of Massachusetts Bay were presented to Plymouth officials. The members of Plymouth's General

Court then ordered the Baptists to stop holding meetings. When Holmes and his followers continued to worship together, they were indicted for disobeying the General Court's order, and commanded to appear before that body.

With determination and single-mindedness akin to that of Roger Williams, Holmes persisted in holding secret meetings. The authorities responded with similar resolve to rid themselves of this dissenter. Holmes was arrested in the middle of a Baptist meeting in the Town of Lynn, Massachusetts. He was fined thirty pounds, and when he refused to pay it he was sent to jail. Three months later, he was taken from the jail, tied to the public whipping post in the center of town and given thirty lashes (one for each pound of the fine). Holmes then moved to Newport and became the minister of the First Baptist Church there.

In the end, then, Newman and Old Rehoboth authorities were victorious in preserving the religious stability of the town. Some years later when a second group of Baptists attempted to form a church in Old Rehoboth, they were again forced from the town but this time found refuge in nearby Swansea.

In the decade beginning with the critical year of 1645, running through the years of controversy with the Baptists and closing with the year 1655, Old Rehoboth went through what one might call the pioneering stage of community development. The working hours of the

The Caleb Williams cottage typifies the settlements of the developing community.

settlers were consumed by the initial hardships and problems of founding a new settlement: dividing, clearing and fencing the land; erecting houses and barns; laying out roads within the township and to Providence and Boston (what later became the famous Boston Post Road, Route 1A, was begun during this period); completing the meeting-house and parsonage: constructing foot bridges across streams; and settling major political disagreements. In short, the future history of Old Rehoboth rested upon foundations laid during this crucial first decade of community life when the inhabitants numbered about two hundred fifty and the population of all the towns in Plymouth Colony amounted to approximately twenty-five hundred.

Of all the projects during these early years, none was more important than the construction of gristmills. We can safely assume that the residents of Old Rehoboth wasted little time in erecting these structures whose importance was rivaled only by the meeting-house. The first gristmill was built by Richard Wright at the falls of Omega Pond in Phillipsdale. The second was built in Rumford on the Ten Mile River (then called the Mill River) at the site of what later came to be named Hunts' Mills, after the family who took over the mill operation in 1713. Powered by water, the mill ground corn and wheat grown by the inhabi-

This postcard scene of the Ten Mile River recalls its role in the community's recreational life. Originally the Mill River, it was the site of the Rumford gristmill in 1713.

tants of the town into meal and flour. The mill was built over a waterway that moved a large wooden wheel which, in turn, rotated a large stone upstairs in the mill. Wheat or corn was placed between the stones, ground into fine meal or flour from which a variety of products (corn meal, bread, puddings, pancakes and later Johnny-cakes, to name a few) were made at home. Seafood, meat from wild animals (turkeys, pheasants, rabbits and the numerous black geese of the area), apples, berries and pumpkins were other important foods.

Sometime after the gristmill was built a saw mill, which converted logs into boards and thus improved the appearance and construction of homes in Old Rehoboth, was erected nearby. This most likely occurred sometime between 1655 and the outbreak of King Philip's War in 1675, a period which marks a second stage of Old Rehoboth's growth when the community began to take on the character and appearance of a more "polished" settlement. The meeting-house, for example, was enlarged and improved during these years, losing much of the barnlike appearance on the outside and containing galleries on the inside. In 1674 the town approved the construction of a new meeting-house which was not completed until 1680. By 1675 there were three garrison houses located in different parts of the settlement. During this period also a small amount of trade with Providence was begun, with Seekonk Cove (Omega Pond) serving as the center of this activity and most likely having a wharf or two.

The passing of the years between 1655 and 1675 saw the lives of some of the town's leading citizens end. In 1662 the aged John Brown died in his sleep at Wannamoisett. A year later Samuel Newman was called to meet his Calvinist God.

Now there remained only one man—Captain Thomas Willett—equal to, if he did not exceed, the stature of these important early leaders of Old Rehoboth. Willett was born in England and, like John Brown and the Pilgrims in general, he moved to Holland where he learned the Dutch language. He came to Plymouth in 1629, and seven years later he married John Brown's daughter. In 1647 Willett replaced Myles Standish as the Captain of the Plymouth militia, and four years later he joined his father-in-law as one of the Governor's assistants.

In 1660, Willett moved to Old Rehoboth and established himself at Wannamoisett. A trusted friend of the Indians and an able negotiator, Willett purchased large tracts of land from the Wampanoags for Plymouth Colony. In addition to Taunton's North Purchase (present day

The Sowams-Rehoboth boundary stone, located at the Silver Spring golf course: Sowams, the Indian for "south land," was the area acquired by Captain Thomas Willett as he pioneered the development of Swansea. Wannamoisett is the Indian for "a good fishing place," and "Rehoboth" is marked on the other side of the stone.

Norton and Mansfield), Willett acquired the deed to Sowams (Indian word meaning the South land) and pioneered the establishment of Swansea on this former Indian land. Furthermore, he was responsible for completing Old Rehoboth's North Purchase. In 1661 he bought from Wamsutta, son of Massasoit, the territory which eventually became Attleboro, North Attleboro and Cumberland and which completed the territorial limits of Old Rehoboth. The townsmen rewarded Willett for his services to Old Rehoboth by voting that he "shall have liberty to take five hundred or six hundred acres of land northward or eastward, beyond the bounds of our town, where he shall think it most convenient for himself."

Willett was shortly called to duty outside the town which resulted in his reputation and prestige spreading far beyond the relatively small worlds of Old Rehoboth and Plymouth Colony. During the 1660's the English government was attempting to wrestle control of New Amsterdam (New York City) from the Dutch, and Willett joined Massachusetts and Plymouth militiamen in Manhattan. His knowledge of the Dutch language put him in good stead once the English gained control of New Amsterdam. Not only did he negotiate a final settlement with the Dutch governor, the famous Peter Stuyvesant, but he was also responsible for organizing the new government of the colony. He won the confidence of both the Dutch and the English, and when the island colony was rechristened New York, Willett was elected its first mayor in 1665. Two years later he was reelected. Finally, he returned to Wannamoisett where he died in 1674.

His death marked the end of an era. Under the leadership of John Brown, Samuel Newman and Willett, Old Rehoboth had made tremendous progress in the approximately thirty years since the town was incorporated. With the rudiments of a future important town in Plymouth Colony now firmly established, the residents of Old Rehoboth could, as the year 1675 began, look backward with pride and forward with confidence. Little did they know, however, that they would soon have to start all over again. Few could have foreseen at the beginning of 1675 that the Indians would soon lay waste to their settlement, forcing these deeply religious Pilgrims and Puritans to reassess their lives and to ask themselves how they had so offended God that He would punish them by using the hand of the red heathen.

Perhaps if John Brown or Captain Willett—two men the Indians trusted and respected—had been alive, King Philip's War would have been delayed. But even Brown or Willett would not have been able to prevent the bloody clash between the English and the Indians. Years of land manipulation and disrespect for Indian rights and lifestyle could be redeemed, King Philip believed, only by the shedding of whitemen's blood.

II
King Philip Seeks Revenge

King Philip's War began in the early summer of 1675 as the inhabitants of Old Rehoboth were busy in their fields, and ended in the early fall of 1676 with many New Englanders lacking homes to live in, let alone crops to harvest. In one respect the war was the bloodiest in American history. When the several thousand whites who were killed are measured against the total population of America at this time (perhaps one hundred thousand people), one is left with a fatality rate which exceeds those of all other American wars. Where people managed to survive, their homes and towns often did not. In the fourteen or so months of the war, fifty-two of the ninety towns spread across New England were attacked, and twelve were destroyed almost completely.

Old Rehoboth was one of this unfortunate dozen. Thus the war left its scars on the area for years to come. It was Old Rehoboth's fate to be in the heart of Wampanoag country, and thus to experience early and intensely the wrath of King Philip's warriors and their allies. Old Rehoboth's men retaliated in kind, and made significant contributions to the defeat and pacification of the Wampanoags on the East Bay and the Narragansetts on the West. For all these reasons, the story of King Philip's War is a significant chapter in the history of New England, Rhode Island and especially the territory which today comprises East Providence.

When the Pilgrims landed in Plymouth in 1620 Massasoit, chief of the Wampanoags of southern New England, befriended the settlers and helped them through their early difficulties in America. From this date

Indian Rock in Kent Heights recalls years when it served as a look-out point during bloody fighting between the colonists and the Wampanoags.

to 1662, the year of Massasoit's death, the Wampanoags were allies of the English, sometimes fighting side-by-side with the white settlers against other Indians. Massaoit attached himself to the English and granted them extensive tracts of land primarily for one reason—protection. Prior to the arrival of the Pilgrims, the Wampanoag villages which stretched from Plymouth to the Seekonk River had been hit with a plague that considerably diminished their numbers. The Wampanoags were now easy prey for their mortal enemy, the Narragansetts, who lived across the Bay. Thus by allying his weakened tribe with the English and deeding them land all around him, Massasoit hoped to create a buffer between himself and the much feared Narragansetts.

As Massasoit and later his son, Wamsutta, completed the land grants which formed the extensive territorial limits of Old Rehoboth, the Wampanoags gradually moved southward toward the Mount Hope peninsula where Philip would soon find himself with his back against the ocean. Indian villages at Pawtucket, Seekonk Cove (present day Philipsdale in East Providence), Watchemoket (the area destined to become the commercial and residential center of East Providence in the late nineteenth and early twentieth centuries) and Wannamoisett (Riverside) had been abandoned and the land sold to Old Rehoboth authorities.

The granting of these areas to the English for nominal sums was part of Massasoit's protective strategy against the Narragansetts. At several points along Narragansett Bay and the Seekonk River in present day East Providence the Wampanoags were particularly vulnerable to an invasion by their enemy. First, where the Bay narrowed near the Pawtuxet and the Gaspee Point area in Warwick, the Narragansetts could easily cross eastward and land at Wannamoisett. Second, the enemy could move northward along the Bay until it narrowed into the Seekonk River, and then cross at Watchemoket or Seekonk Cove. By selling the original eight mile square tract of land upon which Old Rehoboth was built, and by adding the Wannamoisett territory to the settlers' possession, Massasoit had in effect blocked the entry of the Narragansetts into Wampanoag country.

The accommodating policy of Massasoit created a climate of relative peace (with the exception of the Pequot War of 1637) in the decades between the settlement of Plymouth and the beginning of King Philip's War. During these years the Wampanoags lived in small villages on the outskirts of white settlements. Clusters of wigwams were found throughout Plymouth Colony, with the main settlement at Mount Hope to the south of Old Rehoboth. Here the Indians laid out their fields and grew corn, squash and pumpkins. Women were primarily responsible for cultivating the fields, while the men hunted and fished.

The Wampanoags constantly complained to Rehoboth authorities of the inhabitants' disrespect for their lands. In 1651, for example, the Indians protested to town officials that whites were allowing their livestock to trample through Indian fields. Repeatedly the Indians made these and other complaints to John Brown who constantly brought the grievances to the attention of the authorities in Plymouth. Disputes over land often resulted because the Indians did not understand or accept the English notion of land ownership. When the Wampanoags sold land to settlers who did not occupy it immediately, the Indians continued to make use of it. Then when the settlers finally moved onto the land, the Indians sometimes persisted in claiming the right to use it. Hence the term "Indian giver," which is used in reference to someone who takes something back, stems from the land disputes of the seventeenth century.

The death of Massasoit in 1662 came at a time when Indian grievances against and resentment toward the English were mounting. Although the new leaders and younger generation of the Wampanoags continued to pursue outwardly Massasoit's policy of peaceful coexistence with the English, in reality the old chief's accommodating approach to the whiteman died with him. While King Philip would have preferred to act slowly, forging alliances and laying the groundwork for all-out war, events began to get out of control and planned revenge gave way to indiscriminate attacks and killings.

Wamsutta, the oldest son of Massasoit, succeeded his father as chief of the Wampanoags. In a short while Plymouth officials called him to appear before them to answer questions concerning a plot against the whiteman. When the inquiry had finished, Wamsutta went to nearby Marshfield to visit a white settler. Shortly, he became ill, and his braves carried him through the wilderness to his home at Mount Hope where he died. Many Indians came to believe that their chief had been poisoned by whitemen.

Metacomet, better known as Philip, the younger brother of Wamsutta, now became the chief of the Wampanoags. Already hostile to the English, the death of his brother intensified Philip's desire to wage war on the white enemy. But since the Wampanoags numbered only about a thousand, Philip would have to bide his time until he could forge alli-

Metacomet Country Club retains the name of the Wampanoag chief, better known as King Philip, who led his tribe against the English settlers.

ances with the Narragansetts (about 4,000 strong) of Rhode Island and the Nipmucks of central Massachusetts (approximately 3,000 in all). In the meantime, Philip promised suspicious Plymouth officials that he would follow in his father's footsteps and try to maintain peace.

In spite of Philip's pledge, war scares put the people of Old Rehoboth and other towns in the heart of Wampanoag country on the alert throughout the 1660's. In 1667, for example, Philip was again called before Plymouth officials to answer questions concerning a rumored plot against the white settlers. The Indians were forced to turn over their guns to the English. But while there was some evidence of a plot, Philip was simply fined and his braves' guns were returned. Two years later, the opposite side of the Bay was filled with rumors of an impending Indian onslaught. The scare ended as the others had, with Ninigret, a Narrangansett chief, being questioned and then released.

In the early 1670's, however, Indian belligerence became more visible. Residents in Swansea reported seeing armed Wampanoag and Narragansett warriors at Mount Hope. When Philip was called before authorities, he was compelled to give up all his guns and to sign a new peace treaty with the whites. Disarmed and humiliated, Philip returned to Mount Hope determined to push on secretly with his plans for war.

For the next several years affairs in Old Rehoboth and the rest of Plymouth Colony appeared to return to normal. This peaceful surface, however, was broken in 1675 by John Sassamon. This Wampanoag Indian had been raised as a Christian, had studied at Harvard and then had decided to return to his people where he became Philip's secretary. After several years Sassamon left Philip and was called to be a preacher to the Indians at Middleboro in Plymouth Colony.

As Philip's close aide and translator, Sassamon had witnessed at close range the Wampanoag chief's hatred of the whiteman and learned of his plan to restore Indian pride and rights by warfare. In January of 1675, Sassamon told Plymouth authorities of Philip's grand scheme. Several days later, Sassamon was found floating in a pond where he had been thrown after his head was clubbed and his neck broken. Three Indians were tried, convicted and hanged for murder at the beginning of June. War was only days away, for Philip was now afraid that the plot against Sassamon would be traced to him. Reports began to filter in that Wampanoags were armed and in war paint and that they had sent their women and children across the Bay to the safety of Narragansett country.

Swansea, the closest settlement to Mount Hope and the only obstacle in Philip's path to Old Rehoboth, was the first to feel the wrath of the Wampanoags. On the Lord's day June 20, 1675, the Indians began their war of revenge. The Wampanoags attempted to provoke the residents of Swansea into shooting first, because Philip believed that the first side which caused the shedding of blood would lose the war. Thus the Indians robbed and burned homes in Swansea, hoping that the residents would respond with their guns. The Wampanoags were not disappointed; one of them was wounded and now they were prepared to shoot back. June 24th was set aside as a day of fasting and humiliation because of the difficulties with the Indians. Philip's warriors took this opportunity to ransack more dwellings and to attack the residents of Swansea on their way home from church. By the end of the day, nine settlers were dead, a number of others were wounded and several houses were destroyed. Reports and calls for help were sent to Plymouth and Boston. Old Rehoboth began to brace itself for an Indian attack as colonial officials started to prepare for all-out war.

Massachusetts and Plymouth forces were quickly dispatched to Swansea where they united and headed for Mount Hope. By this time, though, Philip had escaped from his campsite, sailed across Mount Hope Bay and the Taunton River and sought temporary refuge with the Pocasset Indians in the Fall River area. The English built a fort at Mount Hope, stationed some of their men there and renewed the pursuit of the Indians. After destroying the Town of Dartmouth, Philip ambushed the English forces, inflicting fifteen casualties, and then made his escape back across the the Taunton River with his sights set on central Massachusetts where he hoped to cause more destruction and killing by enlisting the support of the Nipmuck Indians of that area.

As the people of Old Rehoboth huddled in their garrison houses, Philip led the Wampanoags and Pocassets through the town. The men of Old Rehoboth, commanded by Rev. Noah Newman who had succeeded his father as minister to the people of the town, were joined in their pursuit of Philip by friendly Mohegan Indians from central Connecticut and by volunteers from Providence and Taunton. At a site in present day Burrillville, Rhode Island, they caught up with the Indians and managed to kill over twenty of them. But Philip and his main force escaped into Nipmuck country.

During the early battles of the war, when the Wampanoags seemed to be fighting almost alone, officials in Massachusetts, Plymouth and Rhode Island attempted to neutralize other tribes. Of particular importance were the efforts of New England leaders to seek the assurance of the powerful Narragansetts that they would not join Philip in his war of revenge. With the help of Roger Williams, a meeting was arranged with the Narragansetts who then promised not to aid the Wampanoags. But their actions spoke louder than their words. They began to harbor Wampanoags and Pocassets who were fleeing from battle with the English. It was only a matter of time, then, before the English would make the Narragansetts account for these activities.

From late summer through the fall of 1675 the war shifted to central and western Massachusetts. Philip with his Wampanoag braves and Nipmuck followers attacked towns up and down the Connecticut River Valley. All across this area people were on the alert and in the process of making defensive preparations for war. Watchposts were maintained day and night. Townspeople hurriedly erected fortifications from stones and trees to shelter the inhabitants when the Indians began their assault.

While Philip and his followers were throwing terror into the hearts of the people of central and western New England, the attention of officials in eastern Massachusetts and Connecticut, Plymouth and Rhode Island focused on the behavior of the Narragansetts. The English came to believe that the military successes of the Wampanoags were achieved only because the powerful Narragansetts were aiding them. Late in October of 1675 these suspicions were confirmed when a friendly Indian who had just returned from the Narragansetts' village informed white authorities that Canonchet, their chief, was planning to attack the English. In November the Commissioners of the United Colonies of New England decided to send a one thousand man force to subdue the Narragansetts.

Recruits and volunteers were drawn from Old Rehoboth and other towns in Plymouth Colony and from Massachusetts Bay, Rhode Island and Connecticut. Military and civil leaders began to draw up plans for the single most bloody battle in Rhode Island history—the Great Swamp Fight. By early December troops had begun their trek toward Narragansett country from all over New England. The forces of Plymouth Colony and Massachusetts Bay joined one another at Old Rehoboth on December 9th, ferried across the Seekonk River and began the slow march down the western shore of Narragansett Bay. The journey from Old Rehoboth briefly stopped at Wickford, where the army established its headquarters, and then moved on to link up with the forces from Connecticut for the attack on the Narragansett village in the Great Swamp. The battle resulted in a resounding English Victory but the war was far from over. Indeed, the destruction of the Great Swamp village and the slaughter of several hundred of their men, women and children only intensified the Narragansetts' will to continue fighting.

With Philip still in Nipmuck country in central and western Massachusetts and the Narragansetts attempting to regroup, the Old Rehoboth area and most of southern New England returned to relative peace for the remainder of the winter of 1675-76. But spring brought warfare to the region once again. In mid-March, for example, Warwick and Wickford were burned. Within a short while, the English abandoned almost the entire area on the western shore of Narragansett Bay below Providence.

Plymouth officials sent Captain Michael Pierce of Scituate, Massachusetts with fifty soldiers and twenty friendly Indians to the Narragansett Bay area to do battle with the revenge-seeking natives. On March 25th the Plymouth forces arrived in Old Rehoboth, where they lodged for the night in the Newman Garrison and other homes in the center of town. The following morning, bolstered by recruits from Old Rehoboth, Pierce led his forces toward the Pawtucket River, where he had learned the Indians were located. Anticipating a major battle, Pierce sent a messenger to Providence to secure more men. Unfortunately, the message was not delivered in time, and Pierce with his small force was confronted by a large band of Narragansetts.

The disaster known as "Pierce's Fight" began when the English spotted several Indians and began a chase into the wilderness. All this was by design, for better than five hundred Narragansetts were hiding in the woods prepared to attack Pierce's forces once the decoys brought them to the site of the planned ambush. When the English found themselves surrounded by Indians, they attempted to fight their way free and were almost totally wiped out. Fifty-two whites died (including two residents of Old Rehoboth) and eleven friendly Indians. A handful of survivors, half a dozen at most, retreated to Woodcock's Garrison in the North Purchase while news of the debacle began to spread.

Panic now struck Old Rehoboth. With the numerous Narragansetts nearby and nothing in their path to the town, some residents most likeleft for Aquidneck Island where the towns of Portsmouth and Newport had become secure havens for refugees from Plymouth, Massachusetts and Rhode Island. Those who elected to stay in Old Rehoboth sought the protection of the Newman garrison on the "Ring of the Green." Conditions in garrison houses at times of panic are not difficult to imagine. Although most garrisons, like Old Rehoboth's Newman house, were the largest homes in a town, they were not big enough to hold comfortably the nearly one hundred people who sometimes sought shelter there. In many cases people brought weapons, food and valuable possessions, so that there was scarcely any room to move. Guards were posted day and night and few people dared to go outside. At night sleeping bodies of all ages and both sexes were strewn on the floor in all parts of the house. Doubtless sleepers were awakened by the nightmare screams of children. At other times a suspicious noise outside could stir the sleeping townspeople out of their rest in the middle of the night, only to prove to be a false alarm. In some cases, people spent days and even weeks huddled in a garrison house, watching for signs of Indian activity while praying that an attack would never come.

The nerves of the inhabitants of Old Rehoboth's Newman garrison, however, were not frayed by a long and anxious wait for something to happen. The sound and the fury of the Narragansetts came and passed quickly, and when it was over Old Rehoboth stood no longer. The morning of March 28th, two days after the disaster of Pierce's Fight, dawned bright and crisp with a stiff breeze blowing across the Seekonk plain. The calm of this early spring morning was soon broken by the war cries and gunfire of the Indians. They began to shoot and drive off the cattle and horses of the residents. Next they set fire to the vacant houses. They found one house still occupied, that of a brickmaker named Robert Beers who had refused to join the other settlers at the garrison house. Beers was shot through a window and his house was set ablaze. Gunfire from the people in the garrison house repulsed an Indian attack on that building. As night began to fall, the fear-stricken residents watched helplessly as the "Ring of the Green" went up in smoke. All through the night they peered from their refuge as small fires and smoldering ruins illuminated the darkness.

The next morning, as the ashes continued to send smoke into the sky, the worst fears of the residents were confirmed. There was no town to which they could return. One house besides the Newman Garrison remained standing on the Ring of the Green. Forty houses and nearly as many barns had been destroyed. While the residents took stock of the devastation on March 29th, the Indians directed their anger against Providence where they set fire to thirty dwellings including the home of Roger Williams.

As news of the disasters in Old Rehoboth and Providence spread, people began to abandon other exposed towns nearby. In spite of the offer of Plymouth to relocate the Old Rehoboth people in a more secure area, the residents chose to remain in their settlement and to begin picking up the pieces. At the same time, the Indians seemed to be stronger than ever as attacks continued all over Massachusetts and Plymouth.

These new Indian successes were interpreted by the people of Old Rehoboth, and by New Englanders in general, as signs of God's continuing displeasure with and punishment of them. In the Pilgrim and Puritan view, the hand of God was everywhere. A good harvest, a large healthy family and worldly success were seen as signs of God's pleasure and approval. But God also showed His disapproval of His chosen people's ways through droughts, floods, poor harvests, economic failures and, finally and most importantly, Indian attacks. In short, the sins of New Englanders caused the war.

King Philip was primarily a tool of God for punishing and disciplining the people of the "chosen land." This was why throughout the war authorities attempted to fight the Indians not simply with guns but also with prayers. From the beginning to the end of hostilities, public officials set aside days of humiliation and prayer. On these occasions settlers across .New England would gather in their meeting-houses and go through a breast-beating ritual in which they recounted their many sins, promised repentance and asked God for deliverance from the blood-thirsty red heathen. The spirit of these days of humiliation was caught by Philip Walker, a poet and resident of Old Rehoboth (whose house is still standing in East Providence):

Let's search the Court the Country, town
and City
the Tribe the house the person find 'tis
pity
to miss the knowledge of the thing or things
for which God's angry and His Judgment brings. . .

A side view of the home of Old Rehoboth poet Philip Walker *(see also p. 46)*

In the midst of the war another poet added: "O New England, I understand, with thee God is offended: And therefore he doth humble thee, till thou thy ways hast mended."

Logically, then, towns like Old Rehoboth which were singled out by God for total destruction must have been particularly guilty of offenses against the Lord. Providence was a prime example. It had suffered heavy destruction a day after the Indians had attacked Old Rehoboth, and the reasons for this punishment were perfectly clear to most New Englanders. Was not Providence a hotbed of heresy? Did not the colony founded by the fanatical Roger Williams shelter Baptists, Quakers and other heretical sects? Providence had clearly received what it deserved. But what about Old Rehoboth? It had driven the Baptists out of town and preserved orthodoxy. Its sins, then, were of a different sort from those of Providence.

In the aftermath of the destruction of Old Rehoboth, the task fell to Rev. Noah Newman to explain to his people the sources of God's displeasure with them. The meeting-house was still standing because its proximity to the garrison house prevented the Indians from destroying it. Most likely, as soon as it was safe to leave the garrison, the people of Old Rehoboth filed into the meeting-house where in humiliation they promised to reform their ways. Undoubtedly Newman told them that over the years their greed for riches and land and their formality and indifference to worship and prayer had been increasing until God could no longer tolerate such sins. The war and the destruction of the town, Newman went on to point out, were actually blessings in disguise. Now the people of Old Rehoboth could start all over again and this time follow in the path of righteousness.

Apparently, the residents of Old Rehoboth and of New England in general, had learned their lesson and begun to reform their lives, for in the late spring and early summer of 1676 the tide of the war turned in favor of the English. New England officials formulated a war plan which called for Connecticut forces to move up the Connecticut River Valley towards central and western Massachusetts. They were to be joined there by Massachusetts men who would push from the Boston area westward across the colony. In this way, the two armies with their Indian allies would converge on the enemy's stronghold from two points, destroying crops and villages along the way. In the meantime, Plymouth Colony forces would be on the alert in Wampanoag country around Old Rehoboth, waiting in case the Indians sought refuge there.

As the armies advanced through New England, the Indians began to scatter and prowl the countryside for food. Some of Philip's allies decided to surrender to the English. Encouraged by this action, on June 19th, Massachusetts attempted to break the back of the enemy by issuing a declaration of mercy. Leniency would be granted to Indians who surrendered. Individuals and small groups of Indians, hungry and weary from roaming the wilds for nearly a year, started to lay down their guns. Many tried to exonerate themselves by blaming Philip for forcing the war upon them. By the middle of July, the Nipmucks and Narragansetts were ready to sign a peace treaty with the English. The war would end as it had begun–with Philip and his Wampanoag warriors fighting for the Indian cause alone.

The war would also end where it had begun–in the vicinity of Old Rehoboth. With allies falling all about him, Philip returned to his home in Mount Hope. Once the Plymouth forces made peace with the Pocassets and Sakonnets on the eastern shore of Mount Hope Bay, they were ready to concentrate on finding Philip. Throughout July the Plymouth army hunted down Wampanoags and searched fruitlessly for the by now almost mythical Philip. Even if all the Indians were pacified through surrender or death, the English would not rest until Philip was captured.

Finally, on July 30th the great Wampanoag sachem was spotted attempting to navigate the Taunton River with a group of Indians. A small force of English soldiers prevented the crossing and sent the Indians scurrying into the wilderness. It was clear that Philip would try once again to cross the river in order to return to Mount Hope. The English under the leadership of Benjamin Church now lay in wait. On August 1st the Indians appeared again. Church's men attacked, killing a number of Indians and capturing Philip's wife and son. But once more Philip eluded them.

For the next several days, the English pursued the Indians like hounds on a feverish chase driven by the scent of blood. In desperation the hunted Indians fled to Narragansett Bay and the numerous small islands which would provide temporary security. Philip, however, remained at a secret hiding place on Mount Hope where he might not have been found for weeks had not one of his own braves betrayed him.

On August 11th, the Wampanoag traitor was brought to Benjamin Church and offered to lead the English forces to Philip. With their guides ahead of them, the troops hastened toward Mount Hope. They arrived in the middle of the night and encircled the swamp near Philip's hideout. Their Indian guide directed their attention to the exact location of Philip's shelter. The soldiers now began firing on the sleeping Indians, many of whom died without even waking. Others began to scatter. Philip himself started to run for his life, only to be confronted by a white soldier and an Indian ally. When the whiteman' gun failed him, his Indian companion fired and a figure in the dark slumped to the swampwater below. Upon examining the body, they discovered that Philip had fallen at their feet.

There on his beloved Mount Hope, in the pitch blackness of night lay the bleeding, mudstained, lifeless body of the greatest enemy New Englanders had ever had. In death as in life Philip, like all Indians, appeared to the English more animal than human. Church examined the body of his foe and later wrote that it resembled "a doleful, great, naked, dirty beast." Before Philip's body was decapitated and quartered, the troops gathered around to stare almost in awe at the enemy all New England had feared and pursued for over a year. Many throughout New England would most likely want to get a glimpse of the body of their mortal foe. Thus Church took Philip's head with him, and it was later mounted on a pole in Plymouth for all the curious to see. To the Indian who killed the Wampanoag chief, Church awarded a hand. For years this Indian would carry Philip's hand throughout the area and exhibit it for money.

With the death of King Philip on August 12th there remained only several pieces of unfinished business. Indians continued to be hunted for sport and for profit. During the war the English had turned captured Indians into money. Those who were guilty of killing whites were shot or hanged. But others, especially women and children, were sold into slavery in the West Indies. Others were made servants to English households. Such exploitation of the Indians for profit continued for a time after King Philip's death.

Furthermore, the war could not be officially declared over until Annawan, Philip's war leader who had managed to escape from Mount Hope when Church attacked, was caught. Annawan and perhaps fifty or sixty braves fled to the Old Rehoboth wilderness where they launched attacks on farms in the area. Church set out to destroy the remaining Wampanoags and caught up with Annawan in the easterly woods of Old Rehoboth. The small bands of Wampanoags under Annawan's command gave up without a fight. By September, in spite of occasional raids by a handful of desperate Indians in different parts of New England, the war was over.

Several thousand whites and twice as many Indians had perished. The much depleted native population was now supervised and carefully watched by whites. Indians could not own guns or ammunition, nor could they live wherever they wanted. With the Indians under control, the English now returned to abandoned communities and began the task of rebuilding towns that were partially or totally destroyed. For the people of Old Rehoboth, it would take many years of hard work to restore vitality to their community. But God had blessed them with victory in the war, and with Him on their side they felt equal to the task.

III
Recovery and Revolution

In the middle of 1676, almost exactly three decades after the original "Ring of the Green" had been laid out, a combination of pioneer and more recent families began the work of reconstructing Old Rehoboth. In many respects the inhabitants reenacted the pioneer stage of the town's history. Temporary shelters had to be found until permanent homes could be erected. Barns and fences had to be rebuilt, and the new meeting-house, begun before the War, had to be completed.

While charred ruins of former homesteads remained for years to come, most homes in the center of town were reconstructed by 1680. The house of Philip Walker, for example, was rebuilt by 1679. This landmark, the oldest Rehoboth house still standing, is located at the corner of Massasoit Avenue and North Broadway in East Providence. Like many of the other houses in Old Rehoboth, it was rebuilt by using some of the scorched timber which remained from the original structure. The Robert Abell House, located on Greenwood Avenue, was also rebuilt sometime during the period of recovery from King Philip's War. A new meeting-house joined the Abell house and the other reconstructed homes on the "Ring of the Green." This second public meeting place and church was an imposing structure which helped make the second "Ring of the Green" much more impressive than the first. With three galleries, a steeple and a bell, and the capacity to seat several hundred people easily, the new building was one of the largest and most attractive houses of worship in the area.

The Philip Walker house, at the corner of Massasoit Avenue and North Broadway in East Providence, is the oldest remaining Rehoboth home. It was rebuilt in 1679 after being burned during King Philip's War.

Since the appearance and size of a meeting-house matched the level of development and the population of a settlement, one can infer that the new structure reflected the growth in numbers and physical maturity of the town. By the eve of King Philip's War, the original population of Old Rehoboth had doubled to approximately five hundred people. The war temporarily halted a further increase in the population and may have even caused it to decline as townsmen were killed in battle and some burned out families did not return to Old Rehoboth. But as normalcy was restored, the number of inhabitants began to expand anew, with the population reaching well over 4,000 by 1765.

During the period between King Philip's War and the Revolution, Old Rehoboth experienced a number of political and territorial changes. First, in 1685 Plymouth Colony was divided into two counties. Old Rehoboth and neighboring towns became part of Bristol County while the remainder of the colony formed Plymouth County. Then in 1692 Plymouth Colony and Massachusetts Bay merged, and Old Rehoboth became a town in Bristol County, Massachusetts. In addition a number of new towns were carved from the original territorial wards of Old Rehoboth. Attleboro, for example, was established in 1694 on land that had been a part of the North Purchase. In 1747 another piece of this territory was set off as the Town of Cumberland, Rhode Island. In the same year Barrington was incorporated on land that was originally part of the Wannamoisett Purchase.

The process of town building was similar in each case. Land-hungry settlers would move from the center of settlement to outlying districts where they would be joined by migrants from other communities. As their number grew, these "outlivers" as they were called would gain the right to hire their own minister and build their own meeting-house. The next step was to petition for incorporation as a new town. In this way the territorial limits of Old Rehoboth began to shrink.

The inhabitants of the town, like all farming people, followed the availability of land. With the area around the "Ring of the Green" largely occupied, growing numbers of people looked to outlying districts in Old Rehoboth, if not to new towns, for homesteads. While the area around the "Ring of the Green" remained the population center of the community, by the early seventeenth century people had dispersed to hamlets on the outskirts of the town, foreshadowing the day when East Providence would be composed of a number of villages.

The drift of the expanding population was in two directions: southeast, toward present day Rehoboth and southwest, toward the Watchemoket area. As early as 1709, town officials were forced to take into consideration the needs of these outlying districts. In that year the schoolmaster was obliged to move his school from district to district because the town center, where the school was kept, was not accessible to all inhabitants. The authorities directed that the school be taught at the "Ring of the Green" and "the neighborhood of the east side of the ring," twenty-one weeks; "Palmer's river," fourteen weeks; "Watchemoket neck," thirteen weeks, and "Capt. Enoch Hunt's neighborhood and the mile and a half," nine weeks.

From the amount of school time assigned to each district, one gets a clear picture of the relative importance of each village within the town. The Palmer's River settlement (that is, present day Rehoboth) was the outlying area that had grown the most and would cause the greatest problems for town officials until 1812 when the village and other land on the eastern side would become a separate town called Rehoboth, and the remaining districts would come under the name Seekonk. One hundred years before this split, signs of the trouble which would ultimately lead to separation began to appear.

Since the settlement at Palmer's River was several miles from the meeting-house on the "Ring of the Green," the outlying residents complained that it was a hardship for them to travel to Sunday services. The trek to the meeting-house was especially difficult during the winter when snow covered the countryside and the wind howled through the wilderness and the barren, frozen fields which lay between Palmer's River and the "Ring of the Green." After a better than hour-long hike through the snow, the residents would arrive at the meeting-house chilled and leg weary, only to be forced to sit for two hours while the minister's sermon droned on in seemingly endless fashion. Services now completed, the settlers headed out of the meeting-house to brave the elements and retrace their steps back to Palmer's River.

Under these circumstances, even the most pious individual was tempted to miss Sunday worship. Justifiably, then, in 1711 the inhabitants of the Palmer's River village petitioned the Massachusetts General Court for the right to establish a second church and hire their own minister. The people in the center of the town opposed the petition because the burden of maintaining two ministers and churches would increase the taxes which were levied for the support of religion. After a heated dispute between the eastern and western sections of the town, the General Court granted the Palmer's River settlers the right to hire their own minister in 1713. By 1721 a new meeting-house, the Second Congregational Church of Rehoboth, was completed in that section of town.

Having achieved a measure of religious independence from the town center, the residents of Palmer's River sought to establish their economic autonomy as well. The people most likely built a gristmill so that they would not have to travel to Hunts' Mills on the other side of town to have their corn and wheat ground into meal and flour. Furthermore, along Palmer's River Ebenezer Peck built his blacksmith shop and supplied the iron needs of his neighbors. In short, the Palmer's River settlement had become, to a great extent, a self-sufficient village and was on its way toward developing into a small town (present day Rehoboth) in its own right.

Yet in spite of the growth of this outlying eastern district, the area around the "Ring of the Green" (that is, present day Rumford in East

Providence) remained not only the most heavily populated area in Old Rehoboth for a good part of the eighteenth century, but the religious, political and social center of the town as well. The First Congregational Church (present day Newman Church) in the center of the town was far bigger than the modest Second Church at Palmer's River. Moreover, the meeting-house on the "Ring of the Green" dwarfed its rival building in the other part of town not only in size but in public importance as well. Town meetings and other public gatherings continued to be held in the meeting-house on the "Ring."

Thus if someone had taken an aerial photograph of Old Rehoboth in 1775, as the Revolution was about to begin, it would have revealed both change from and continuity with the original pattern of settlement. In the northwestern part of the town (Rumford), there would have appeared a large number of homes, barns and fields spreading out from the meeting-house and "Ring of the Green." Looking west, one would have seen several wharves, ships and boats along the Seekonk River, presenting a picture of moderate commercial activity.

Following the Seekonk River south toward Watchemoket one would have discovered the outlines of a small farming and fishing area extending into Wannamoisett (Riverside). Finally, looking toward the east one would have seen a tiny, bustling hamlet in the area of Palmer's River, and homesteads scattering northward throughout what is present day Rehoboth. The residents of these diverse districts were about to bury their differences and disagreements and to unite in a common cause against their mother country.

After defending her colonies in an expensive seven year war with the French and Indians, the British government hoped when a peace treaty was signed in 1763 to begin to replenish much of its depleted treasury by taxing the Americans, and by rigidly enforcing existing trade regulations. But over the decades a British policy of neglect had conditioned Americans to freedom from outside interference in colonial affairs. British customs officials vigorously enforced trade regulations and customs levies which disrupted American sea trade. And, of course, colonial trade was centered in New England and principally in Massachusetts and Rhode Island. For this reason, these two colonies would be the first to protest the continuing British interference in the American economy.

This opposition led to one of the most famous events in Rhode Island history—the burning of the Gaspee. To avoid customs ships on the open waters of Narragansett Bay, Rhode Island merchants had turned to the numerous coves along the shoreline where under the cover of night they unloaded their cargoes of contraband. On June 9, 1772, while searching for such illegal activity, the customs sloop Gaspee ran aground just below Providence at present day Gaspee Point in Warwick. A group of men boarded the ship and, after wounding the commander and disarming the crew, set the Gaspee on fire. This incident was more serious than the burning of the Liberty because an officer of the King was wounded and his men were held at gun point.

The Royal government therefore issued a proclamation which offered a reward for information on the participants in the burning of the Gaspee. A commission which included the governor of Rhode Island was also formed to investigate the incident. As almost everyone knew, the destroyers of the Gaspee were well-to-do men. The conspirators consisted of successful merchants of Providence, including the wealthy John Brown, and at least one important resident of Old Rehoboth. Robert Sutton, whose descendants later became a prominent family in East Providence, joined with his Providence neighbors in destroying the Gaspee. Neither Sutton nor the others were ever punished for their actions. The people and government of Rhode Island protected them, and British officials were unable to gather sufficient evidence for conviction.

Less than a year later Old Rehoboth, like all of Massachusetts, was caught up in the revolutionary fervor which followed British reaction to the Boston Tea Party. The British government responded with the "Intolerable" Acts which, among other things, closed the Port of Boston and altered the government of Massachusetts by making previously elected representatives subject to appointment by the King and royal governor. This last provision was probably the most serious threat to American political liberty to date. Thus Committees of Correspondence, which had been formed to coordinate boycotts in the 1760's, once again sprang to action up and down the Atlantic Coast.

In the summer of 1774, for example, Old Rehoboth's six man committee–comprised of Ephraim Starkweather, Nathan Daggett, Thomas Carpenter 3rd, John Lyon, Joseph Bridgham and William Cole–began to report to its sister body in Boston the actions of the town in support of the American cause. On July 25th an Old Rehoboth town meeting "Voted not to purchase any goods, imported from Great Britain after the 31st day of August next, until the act for blocking up the harbour of Boston be repealed, and the government be restored to its former privileges." A short while later the First Congregational Church of Old Rehoboth (that is, the present day Newman Church of East Providence) donated six pounds "for the relief and support of the poor of Boston, sufferers by means of the Boston Port Bill."

Throughout the fall of 1774 Old Rehoboth contributed both money and representatives to the Massachusetts provincial congress, an extra-legal body which acted as a state government. On the suggestion of Massachusetts, the first Continental Congress met in Philadelphia in September. Twelve of the thirteen colonies were represented and the delegates voted to establish a Continental Association which would ensure that there would be no trade with England until American grievances were redressed.

But it began to appear that such peaceful action would not be enough to make American resistance successful. Already in late 1774 Massachusetts and other colonies had started to collect and store arms. It was the pursuit of such arms caches that sent British General Thomas Gage on his way to Concord and his historic rendezvous at Lexington with "the shot heard 'round the world." Before arriving at Concord, Gage met armed resistance at Lexington, but the Americans were unable to prevent Gage from reaching his destination and destroying guns and ammunition.

Calls now went out to other Massachusetts towns for minutemen—the citizen soldiers of the Revolution who were trained to answer an alarm, trade pitch fork for rifle, and be ready to do battle in a minute. On April 19th Old Rehoboth sent five companies of minutemen racing toward Lexington-Concord. They were led by seven captains: Samuel Bliss, Phanuel Bishop, Nathaniel Carpenter, Isaac Burr, John Lyon, Jesse Perrin and John Perry. Reinforcements from other towns closer to the battle scene arrived in time to engage the British on their way back to Boston.

The aroused companies of minutemen began firing upon the redcoats from behind fences and trees. When the shooting stopped, Gage counted two hundred seventy-three of his men dead or wounded. The patriots, on the other hand, suffered only about ninety casualties. With the smell of gunfire still in the air and wounded Americans and British corpses lying about the village, the minutemen of Old Rehoboth marched into Lexington. Because of the distance they had to travel, they just missed participating in the opening battle of the American Revolution. But in the months ahead they would find other opportunities to fight for American liberty.

A little more than a month after the Battle of Lexington-Concord, Old Rehoboth began to lay the groundwork for the protection of its people. On May 26, 1775 the town meeting "Voted to raise two companies in this town to be ready on any special alarm; one company to be raised in the westerly part, and the other in the easterly part of said town." Each company consisted of fifty men, several officers and a horse cart which would carry the baggage and supplies of the minutemen when they were called to fight in another town. Dressed in simple homespun clothes, often tattered, dirty and unshaven – the result of days of marching and fighting in the New England countryside – the American farmers turned minutemen soldiers contrasted sharply with the well-disciplined British forces decked out in red uniforms with silver buttons and trim.

But on one score the American farmers outmatched the enemy. Years of experience with guns made most minutemen expert marksmen. While muskets were no longer employed in warfare with Indians, they were used for hunting. Undoubtedly, just about every Old Rehoboth home had a musket hanging over the fireplace. Moreover, colonial law provided that able bodied men from sixteen to sixty serve in the local militia and be supplied with a musket and ammunition. Days of muster were set aside on which an entire town would gather on the green to watch local men march and practice firing their muskets. Thus the Americans' familiarity with guns paid off well during the Revolution.

On the same day it voted to raise two companies of minutemen, Old Rehoboth started to store provisions and ammunition. These supplies were divided between the western ("Ring of the Green") section of town and the eastern (Palmer's River) area. The Revolution now built up a full head of steam. The time was fast approaching when, as John Adam's wife would write from nearby Braintree, "the constant roar of the cannon" would make it difficult to "eat, drink, or sleep." Boston and its outlying towns were in such dire straits that other Massachusetts communities were called on for humanitarian assistance. On June 12, 1775, for example, the Old Rehoboth town meeting "Voted that the selectmen provide for the poor of the town of Boston, that are, or shall be, sent to this town, upon the town's credit."

Less than a week later the most bloody battle of the war occurred at Boston, most likely necessitating further aid from Old Rehoboth and other towns. At Bunker Hill on June 17 four hundred Americans and one thousand British were either killed or wounded. If any had doubted after the Battle of Lexington-Concord that war had arrived, Bunker Hill dispelled their uncertainty. The people of Old Rehoboth, Providence and other towns on the shores of Narragansett Bay became particularly uneasy. These communities were especially vulnerable to attack by British warships which had crowded Newport harbor since the beginning of 1775.

Even before the battles of Lexington-Concord and Bunker Hill, British naval officers had begun to release their hatred of the defiant Americans by frequently directing cannon balls to the Newport shore and by firing upon privateers in the Bay. With little difficulty these warships could level Newport (as they eventually did between 1776 and 1778 when they occupied the seaport) and sail up the Bay, visiting death and destruction on coastal towns as they passed and not stopping until they traveled as far north as the Providence and Seekonk Rivers.

After the Battle of Bunker Hill the British navy began to increase its harassment of the people of Newport. This started a mass exodus of residents who were replaced in the seaport by American soldiers sent to prevent the British from confiscating livestock and other provisions to feed their troops. Just the threat of naval attack had made Newport a ghost town, as people fled to more secure inland areas.

To avert a similar panic-induced evacuation in the upper regions of Narragansett Bay and to fortify their towns against possible attack, officials of Providence and Old Rehoboth authorized the construction of defensive fortifications. Residents quickly erected forts at Field's Point and Fox Point in Providence and at Hog Pen Point (now called Bold Point) in Old Rehoboth (now in East Providence). Old Rehoboth purchased ammunition and other war supplies and mounted four cannons at its fortification. From this elevated fort at Hog Pen Point one could scan the Bay far and wide. The town built an earthwork fortification with a trench from which riflemen could fire upon the enemy below. Old Rehoboth's "Fort Hill" and the other fortifications at Field's Point and Fox Point presented formidable obstacles to the British who were wise enough not to test them.

As the historic year 1776 began, two wartime activities occupied much of the business of Old Rehoboth town meetings – the manufacture of saltpeter used in gunpowder and recruitment for the Continental Army. On February 12, 1776 the town voted "to encourage the manufacturing of salt petre in private families, by affording them the materials they can get without doing damage." Saltpeter was also manufactured in the recently burned out Old Stone House on Roger Williams Avenue in present day East Providence.

The old Cove Factory on Roger Williams Avenue was the site of munitions manufacturing during the Revolutionary War and the War of 1812.

Next, the town dealt with the issue of recruitment for the Continental Army which George Washington had begun to organize in the fall of 1775. Enlistments in the army were for a specified period of time (usually a year, although in some cases as short as three months or as long as three years) and recruits were to be paid a bounty. Colonies were assigned quotas which would have to be filled by a draft if enough volunteers were not found. If one were drafted and had money, a substitute could be hired in one's place.

Old Rehoboth began its recruitment of soldiers in April of 1776. The town voted "to raise a bounty of £ 20 to every soldier that shall enlist into the continental army for three years, or during the war, provided they enlist into the said army within ten days." During the next two years the town extended the bounty in new recruitment drives. Throughout the war the Continental Army varied in strength from a few thousand to as many as twenty-seven thousand. Their efforts in a particular region were supplemented by local companies of minutemen.

Old Rehoboth, like all towns which supported the Revolutionary cause, assumed other wartime responsibilities beyond the recruitment of men and the manufacture of saltpeter. Clothing for soldiers was purchased with town money. Quotas of food, principally meat, to feed soldiers were allotted to towns, and Old Rehoboth had to raise money to purchase more than forty-two thousand pounds of beef. In addition, the families of soldiers who had enlisted in the Continental Army had to be provided for. With their husbands and fathers away, women and children had to cultivate farm land and harvest crops. Undoubtedly, neighbors formed groups to aid the families of Old Rehoboth's Continental soldiers. A special town committee was formed to look after these families and money was set aside in the treasury to meet their needs.

While all of this activity was occurring on the local level, the Continental Congress was meeting in Philadelphia to coordinate the war effort. It became increasingly clear to this body and to many Americans in the spring of 1776 that complete independence from England was the order of the day. Rhode Island became the first colony to throw off the shackles of the British imperial system when on May 4, 1776 the smallest colony declared its independence. The residents of nearby Old Rehoboth, however, would have to wait until the Continental Congress issued its Declaration of Independence two months later.

The first year of the war had now passed and for New Englanders the worst was behind them. Except for the continuing occupation of Newport and sporadic raids on towns along Narragansett Bay (Bristol and Warren were attacked in May of 1778, for example) the area saw little further evidence of the enemy. Old Rehoboth minutemen answered many alarms in Rhode Island, but the scenes of the major battles of the war had shifted to the middle and southern states.

Even the Battle of Rhode Island, which was planned as an important American offensive in the summer of 1778, failed to develop into a major encounter. This ill-fated battle in which a number of Old Rehoboth men lost their lives grew out of the French-American Alliance treaty signed early in May. Almost immediately Washington and Admiral d'Estaing of France developed a land-sea strategy to break the British stranglehold on Newport and Narragansett Bay. The plan called for d'Estaing to approach Newport by sea and land his troops, while a strong American force would land at the opposite end of Aquidneck Island forming a pincers from which the British could not escape. The offensive was launched in late July, and the French ships approached Newport as General John Sullivan led his forces from Providence to Tiverton. At this point Sullivan and the French officers began to quarrel and the campaign came to a standstill.

News now arrived that another British fleet was headed for Newport. d'Estaing proceeded to reembark his troops and set his sails for the advancing British fleet. As the French and British warships approached one another a hurricane-like storm interrupted what could have been a major battle. When calm finally returned to the waters, both fleets were seriously damaged and scattered over miles of ocean. In order to regroup, the British sailed for New York and the French headed for Boston.

The Continental regiments and the local militia of Old Rehoboth and other Massachusetts and Rhode Island towns under Sullivan's command now found themselves abandoned to do battle with the British alone. The American troops, which included a black regiment under Colonel Christopher Greene (a cousin of Rhode Island's famous General Nathaniel Greene), fought bravely, but they were pushed back to the Sakonnet River in Portsmouth. From this point Sullivan ferried his remaining forces to safety in Bristol and Tiverton. Two hundred forty-one Americans (many of them Old Rehoboth men) were dead, wounded or missing, and the British had suffered an equal number of casualties.

In spite of the disaster of this first joint French-American effort, the military power of France, when combined with the determination of local militia men and Continental soldiers, gradually tipped the military scales in favor of the Revolutionaries. By the fall of 1778 the British were forced to end their nearly three year occupation of Newport. Although a peace treaty was not signed until 1783, in reality hostilities came to an end in October 1781 when the British surrendered at Yorktown in Virginia.

In relationship to its size Old Rehoboth made a solid contribution to the patriot victory. More than fourteen hundred men served in the war. All except a handful of these fought as minutemen and answered alarms in various parts of New England. Old Rehoboth minutemen even served under George Washington at the Battle of White Plains in New York. Three hundred ten of the town's men fought in the Continental Army, and thirty-seven of these became officers. Old Rehoboth's men not only fought but they died (especially in the Battle of Rhode Island) for the American cause. Others were captured and imprisoned either in England or on jail ships which were stationed off the Atlantic Coast during the war. The graves of many of the first patriots of the United

The Samuel Newman stone at Newman Cemetery, the church in the background

The Howland stone at Little Neck Cemetery marks the resting place of Mayflower Pilgrim Elizabeth Tilley Howland.

States may be found today in the historical burial grounds of East Providence—Newman, Hunt, Carpenter and Little Neck Cemeteries. But the memory of these patriots is preserved by more than weather-beaten gravestones. Indeed, nothing less than a free and independent United States of America stands as the monument commemorating their lives.

The American Revolution did not end with the war. Tremendous problems which called for revolutionary changes confronted the victors. The ending of any war requires economic adjustment and the Revolution was no exception. A scarcity of hard currency during the war had compelled states to print massive amounts of paper money. A high rate of inflation resulted from the issuance of "cheap" money. Then, too, the national and state governments had borrowed money during the war which had to be repaid. But the Congress formed under the Articles of Confederation had neither the power to lay nor collect taxes. In fact, the Congress did not even have money to pay the soldiers of the Continental Army.

Heavily agricultural towns, like Old Rehoboth, were the hardest hit by post-war economic conditions. During the war farmers in general had experienced relative prosperity. American, French and even English forces provided a ready market for any surplus farm products that were produced. By the mid-1780's, however, this market was no longer available. Farmers now had difficulty paying debts incurred during the war. Creditors began to foreclose on farm mortgages. Moreover, state governments started to raise taxes and to require their payment in specie (coined money, either silver or gold) not in depreciated paper currency.

In Rhode Island and Massachusetts the plight of farmers was particularly harsh. In 1786 the Rhode Island General Assembly, after considerable pressure from farmers, issued paper currency only to have merchants refuse to accept it as payment for debts or purchases. The legislature even passed a law (later ruled unconstitutional) that provided fines for those who refused to honor the currency. In Massachusetts, Daniel Shays became the leader of the farmers' protest and initiated a short-lived rebellion which focused on the courts which had begun foreclosure proceedings.

By and large the residents of Old Rehoboth were supporters of Shays' Rebellion. Like Shays' followers in western Massachusetts, the people of Old Rehoboth first relied upon peaceful conventions of farmers as a means of protest. On June 19, 1786, at the height of Shays' Rebellion, the residents of Old Rehoboth voted "to choose a committee to meet with other towns' committees in the county of Bristol, in a county convention, to consult on the rights of the people of said commonwealth, and to petition the General Court for redress of grievances, or to take any other measures that the convention, when met, shall judge to be the right of the people of this commonwealth." Phanuel Bishop, Frederick Drown and William Daggett were selected to represent the town.

When the Massachusetts legislature ignored the complaints made by the county conventions, the protest took a violent turn. Farmers began to arm themselves, and the Shaysites attempted to gain control of federal arsenals. By the late fall of 1786, civil war seemed imminent in Massachusetts. On December 25th the people of Old Rehoboth voted "that they wished to have an alteration in the present system of government in the commonwealth of Massachusetts. . ." This vote was carried by a majority of one hundred ten.

Finally, in January, open warfare began as Massachusetts militia initiated a campaign to crush Shays' Rebellion. By the end of February, Shays had fled to Vermont and his supporters were in disarray. Peace was restored to Massachusetts. In March supporters of the rebellion in Old Rehoboth gave up their arms and took an oath of allegiance to Massachusetts.

It was now evident to many moderate and conservative leaders that the problems of the post-war years, and in particular Shays Rebellion, stemmed from the weakness of the government which was formed under the Articles of Confederation. Nothing less than a new Constitution which gave a national government considerable power could prevent further turmoil and preserve the hard fought victory of the Revolutionaries. Thus throughout the summer of 1787 the Constitutional Convention met in Philadelphia. By the fall a document outlining a new government was ready to be presented to the states for ratification. Old Rehoboth sent three delegates–Phanuel Bishop, Frederick Drown and William Windsor – to the Massachusetts Convention which ratified the Constitution early in 1788. In contrast to Massachusetts' speedy adoption of the Constitution, Rhode Island, which had been the first to declare independence, was the last to join the Union. Not until May 1790, after the new government had begun operating, did Rhode Island ratify the Constitution.

Peace now settled over both sides of the Seekonk River and ushered in a period of tremendous growth. In the decades ahead what remained of Old Rehoboth would be fashioned into three townships. And in the midst of America's Civil War Old Rehoboth's economic, social and cultural bond with the smallest state, which had been growing for years, would be legally consummated by the incorporation of the most important part of the town as East Providence, Rhode Island.

IV
Division, Local and National, 1790-1865

During the post-Revolutionary decades the expansion of social, economic and cultural intercourse between Providence on one side of the Seekonk River and Old Rehoboth on the other was facilitated by the construction of bridges. Until 1793 tidal ferries at Watchemoket and at a point further north on the Seekonk River (the site of the old Red Bridge) provided the principal means of travel between the two towns. These ferries were powered by the tides which propelled them

This old postcard view from Fort Hill shows the bridges, railroad lines, the Oyster House and a small portion of Watchemoket Square, all the development of the later 19th century.

John Brown's bridge, dedicated to George Washington in 1793, was one of the first to span the Seekonk, replacing the early tidal ferries that shuttled between Old Rehoboth and Providence. The original dedication is incorporated into this plaque, located on the present-day Washington Bridge.

along guide ropes. When not in use, the ropes were lowered under the water to allow boats to pass. This method of crossing the river involved a number of problems. The most obvious one was presented by nature. During poor weather the tidal ferries were unable to operate, stranding travelers in both Old Rehoboth and Providence.

The replacement of the tidal ferries by bridges was thus a major advance in transportation with important consequences for the future of both towns. In 1793 John Brown, the wealthy merchant of India Point, built a bridge connecting Providence with Old Rehoboth at Watchemoket. This structure became not only the means for a growing interchange between the two communities, but for John Brown it was a monument symbolizing the successful closing of the Revolutionary era. Appropriately, Brown named the new bridge after the man most admired by Americans of this period – George Washington. On a marble slab near the bridge Brown had the following inscribed: "Washington Bridge Built by John Brown, Esq., 1793, this monument is erected by the founder and proprietor of India Point as a testimony of high respect for the great illustrious Washington."

The structure spanning the Seekonk was the first covered draw bridge in America. Its roofs and walls resembled a red barn and protected travelers from the weather. More important, however, the rustic exterior of the bridge was designed so that water-shy horses would assume that they were simply walking through a barn rather than crossing a river.

The importance of the Washington Bridge was enhanced by the fact that it was on the famous Boston Post Road. This well-known highway of American history was the primary land route for travelers coming from Maine, New Hampshire and the Boston area and heading south to Connecticut, New York, New Jersy, Pennsylvania, Washington and the states below the Mason-Dixon Line. The Boston Post Road ran through Old Rehoboth (Route 1A in present day East Providence) to Watchemoket. At this point Washington Bridge extended the well-traveled artery across the river. Like the other bridges on the route, one had to pay a toll to cross from Watchemoket to Providence. The toll house was located on the Old Rehoboth (that is, East Providence) side of the Washington Bridge.

Just north of John Brown's bridge stood the Central Bridge constructed by his brother, Moses. This toll bridge was opened on April 9, 1793, three days before the Washington Bridge began transporting

goods and people, and reflected a deep rivalry between the two brothers. They disagreed, for example, on religion. John was a Baptist and Moses had converted to the Quaker faith. With regard to slavery and the slave trade, John had been deeply involved in both, while Moses had managed to change his early proslavery connections and become one of the leading anti-slavery reformers in New England.
slavery reformers in New England.

The bridges of both Browns were destroyed by flood waters in 1807. They were rebuilt only to be wrecked by a hurricane in September 1815. Again necessity required that they be reconstructed, for the bridges had become vital to the lives of people on both sides of the Seekonk River.

A year after the Washington and Central Bridges opened the Baptists built their first church in the center of town. For a number of years Baptist societies had existed in outlying districts. During the middle of the eighteenth century, for instance, at least three Baptist groups of worshipers were formed in the Palmer's River area in the eastern section of Old Rehoboth. Not until 1794, however, when the First Baptist Church was formed did the people of this faith have a house of worship in the center of town.

A new Congregational meeting-house appeared a short while later. Completed in 1810, this fourth building to house the Congregational church is still standing and serving the parishioners of East Providence's Newman Church. The old church built in 1717 was demolished and some of its timber was soon to be used in the construction of a new town hall.

Beneath these outward signs of growth in the years after the Revolution, trouble was brewing in Old Rehoboth which would divide the community into separate towns. At a meeting in 1795 a motion was offered to petition the Massachusetts General Court to establish the western region of Old Rehoboth as a separate town. The motion was defeated, but a little more than a decade later it was revived and, as a result of the "Fighting Town Meeting," the western section of Old Rehoboth was incorporated as Seekonk.

In May 1811, as green was steadily overtaking brown in the countryside of Old Rehoboth, and as the first spring crops began to push through the ground, the attention of the town's farmers was diverted from their fields to the meeting-house. On May 13th a town meeting was called to decide whether Old Rehoboth should send one representative to the General Court in Boston, as had been the practice in the past, or five, an innovation begun a year earlier. When the question was put to a vote by a show of hands, it was unclear which side prevailed.

As one can well imagine, town meetings were often raucous affairs. Frequently, it was difficult for the chairman of the board of selectmen (town council) to be heard above the din of four to five hundred men, many of whom were chewing tobacco and would sometimes, in the heat of argument, forget they were in the meeting house and spit their foul juice on the floor (and, occasionally, perhaps, at an opponent). Then, too, the farmers of Old Rehoboth usually came to the meeting directly from their fields and did not take the time to clean dirt and mud from their boots. Intermixed with the smell of tobacco and manure was the scent of whiskey. On occasion, fists would fly and a cut lip or bloody nose was not uncommon.

All of these elements appear to have been present at the "Fighting Town Meeting" of 1811. To gain control of the gathering and to clarify the vote, it was suggested that individuals who supported sending one representative clasp hands with those who favored electing five and march out of the building in pairs. These votes would be counted, and then the remaining unpaired voters in the meeting-house would show which side had won. When it appeared that the one representative supporters had gained the upper hand, Elkanah French, chairman of the board of selectmen and one of the five-town representatives now in danger of losing his political position, interrupted the proceedings and tried to block the will of the townspeople by claiming the vote was incorrect. With the nearly six hundred voters who had filed out of the building now returning, mass confusion reigned and the meeting was dissolved.

The following day a new meeting was called for May 18th. Emotions already seething were allowed to burn to a white heat in the interval between town meetings so that May 18th witnessed a spectacle which, in violence and acrimony, outstripped the riotous affair of May 13th. As soon as motions to send one representative and five were presented, Elkanah French attempted to assert his authority over the meeting. "I will hear none of your motion and I will put (move) none of your motions" he thundered from the front of the meeting-house. "I will manage this meeting according to my own mind. If you do not like my proceedings, or if I do wrong, prosecute me; bring in your votes for from one to five representatives."

Fist fights now broke out. Bodies crashed against pews, causing some damage to the interior of the meeting-house. French narrowly missed the clenched fist of one enraged resident of Old Rehoboth. In the midst of all this confusion, the townsmen began to vote. After about twenty-five ballots were cast, however, French halted the election and announced that he and four others (all but one of which were already representatives) were elected. The high-handed tactics of French were protested to the Massachusetts General Court which voided the election results and left Old Rehoboth without a representative in 1811.

But French was not about to concede defeat. He requested that the General Court separate Old Rehoboth into two towns, with the western precinct (present day East Providence and Seekonk) forming a new community. On February 3, 1812 the town voted overwhelmingly (328 to 18) against the proposed division and chose two men to make their wishes known to the General Court, and to try to influence that body not to approve French's recommendation. Like French, however, the legislature ignored the wishes of the people and on February 26, 1812 it passed an act granting a charter to a new town called Seekonk (hereafter referred to as Old Seekonk).

All of this political maneuvering during 1811-12 was not uncommon for the times; nor, for that matter, was the thwarting of local popular will by the General Court a phenomenon unique to Rehoboth. In fact, as local communities in Massachusetts began to industrialize, a separation of interests developed in which mill owners were arrayed against anti-industrial agricultural elements in many towns. By appealing over the heads of townspeople to the General Court, industrial interests were able to bring about divisions in which industrial-agricultural town precincts were separated from strictly agricultural areas. Such was most likely the case in Old Rehoboth where mills had already sprung up along the Ten Mile and Seekonk Rivers. The Old Central Mills of East Providence, for example, date from this period.

To be sure, small mills were also found in the eastern section of Old Rehoboth at this time. One thinks of the Rehoboth Union and Orlean Manufacturing Companies, established in 1809 and 1810, respectively. But the availability of water power in the western precinct of Old Rehoboth, which became Old Seekonk in 1812, made that region a more important industrial area. Indeed, in 1828 the growth of mills in this locality would lead to yet another split as the northwestern corner of Old Seekonk was incorporated as part of a new mill town named Pawtucket.

Not only most of Old Rehoboth's industry but also a sizeable portion of its population became part of Old Seekonk in 1812. While Rehoboth was to remain largely agricultural, Old Seekonk would grow in economic, social and cultural diversity between 1812 and 1862. Then another division would disembowel the town as its vital institutions and areas were incorporated under the name East Providence, Rhode Island.

Before that, though, Old Seekonk experienced fifty years of steady expansion, interrupted only by the War of 1812. The town, like all of New England, suffered because British control of the Atlantic hindered sea trade. In July 1814, the British even managed to blockade Narragansett Bay and capture several Providence ships heading for New York. This aroused the people to action, and the old Revolutionary fortifications on both sides of the Bay, including Fort Hill in Old Seekonk, were readied for battle. But the British fleet did not advance and by the end of 1814 the war was over. The people of America could now devote full time to winning the west, introducing the machine or enslaving the blacks. A price would be paid for each preoccupation and the last would exact the highest toll.

In the year the war ended and Americans returned to their enterprising ways, Old Seekonk completed a new town hall. No longer was the meeting-house the scene of public assemblies. Because Congregationalists were now a minority in the town, political and religious affairs had become divorced, although the legal disestablishment of the church did not occur in Massachusetts until 1833. The town hall was the civic center of Old Seekonk and the First Congregational (Newman) Church simply served its parishioners.

The cultural life of Old Seekonk revolved around what later became the East Providence Free Library. The origins of this institution, one of the oldest libraries in the State of Rhode Island, date back to the early years of the American Revolution. In 1772 a group of Rehoboth residents pooled their books and began to meet in the home of Dr. Joseph Bridgham where they exchanged and discussed particular works. When the war started the books were placed in the hands of the women members who called themselves "The Ladies Reading Society." Volumes were placed in a trunk and moved from house to house for meetings. When the trunk became too heavy to carry a permanent meeting place was arranged. The Aldrich House in Rumford, and then the town hall nearby, housed the Society. By this time, the women had changed their group's name to the Female Benevolent Library Society and successive-

The Bridgham Farm windmill is a landmark of an institution as well as a family, for in Dr. Joseph Bridgham's home the community pooled and exchanged books. From these origins grew the East Providence Free Library, one of the oldest in the state.

ly to the Female Library Society, The Seekonk and East Providence Library Association, and finally the East Providence Free Library.

During the decades before the incorporation of East Providence, the town hall housed not only the Library Society but also the contemporary equivalent of a high school. Since the town had no public high school (East Providence High dates from the 1880's), the Seekonk Classical Institute supplied post grammar school education to the few who sought it. Classes met in the town hall and graduates of the Institute often went to college, usually Brown or Harvard.

Town meetings were generally peaceful after the split of 1812. Financial support for education, highway construction and the poor were the main issues confronting the voters each year. In contrast to modern municipal budgets, town expenses in the pre-Civil War decades were miniscule. In 1812, for example, the budget called for four hundred dollars for schools and nine hundred dollars for support of the poor and incidentals. By 1826 the budget had grown considerably, but it was still small and uncomplicated:

Schools	$ 700
Support of Poor and other Town Expenses	$1700
Repair of Highways and Bridges	$2000

These three categories remained the major areas of town expenses up to the Civil War when money for recruits became another costly item.

For recreation, the pre-Civil War inhabitants of Old Seekonk found abundant opportunities for swimming, fishing, clamming and hunting. In addition, the town was a center for two other popular pastimes – canoeing and horse racing. Canoes were found up and down the Seekonk and Ten Mile Rivers. While canoers tried to outdistance one another on water, horses raced on nearby land. The area around present day East Providence was particularly suited for this popular sport. Dr. Timothy Dwight, president of Yale College, visited the area while traveling about New England and described what he saw:

> *Before we reached Providence, we crossed the Seekonk plain, an absolute level, about 5 miles in length and 3½ in bredth. This spot has for a long time been a favorite scene of the Rhode Island horse races; and more than any other ground within my knowledge resembles Hempstead plain on Long Island; devoted from an earlier period to the same miserable employment.*

Eventually, the establishment of Narragansett Race Track on a portion of the Seekonk Plain would continue a tradition begun in colonial times.

Perhaps the favorite spot of pre-Civil War residents of Old Seekonk was Hunts' Mills, the site of the old grist mill on the Ten Mile River. Saw and fulling mills had been added to the location and just prior to the Civil War a cotton mill was opened. Yet in spite of all this activity, Hunts' Mills was one of the most beautiful locations for miles around. Water cascaded over the gristmill dam and jostled against the rocks below, creating a picture book scene for visitors who rested under the shade of nearby trees and drank of nature's beauty. Foot bridges crossed the water above and below the dam, and if strollers wished they could observe the men in the mills plying their trades.

The falls at Hunts' Mills

Campers, weekend picnickers and lovers all found Hunts' Mills to be an ideal place for their activities. Perhaps the most famous visitor to the peaceful retreat was Bristol, Rhode Island's famous General Ambrose Burnside, who would soon distinguish himself in the Civil War. Like other less famous men and women, the General would frequently go by carriage or on horseback for a ride around the countryside and stop for rest and reflection at Hunts' Mills. Other more romantically minded visitors held hands or embraced on an elevated rock (called Sunset Rock) where they watched the sun descend in the west and, overwhelmed with feeling, whispered to one another the words which lovers of all ages have spoken.

In contrast to the leisurely atmosphere of Hunts' Mills, much of the rest of Old Seekonk in the 1830's, '40's and '50's was a beehive of activity as industry grew in the town. Mills dotted the banks of the Ten Mile

An old postcard view of the mouth of the Ten Mile River, with the Cove Factory on the right (shown also on p. 54)

River which was appropriately called the Mill River. The Cove Factory, for instance, one of the more important manufacturers of cotton cloth, was located at Mill River Falls and contained 3,000 spindles, 72 looms and 60 employees. Other, smaller operations were found nearby.

Soon the roar of the steam locomotive joined with the constant

Riverside Square and the railroad station as they appeared on a postcard at the turn of the century

hum of cotton mills to assure the residents of Seekonk that the industrial revolution had come to their once peaceful agricultural town. The Boston and Providence Railroad extended its line down through Old Seekonk in 1831. Steam powered cars were not immediately available. Instead, horse drawn carriages which individuals had to supply for themselves were mounted on the tracks. By 1835, however, steam driven vehicles had arrived in Old Seekonk. The Boston and Providence line ran from Watchemoket northeast toward Attleboro and ended in Boston. In due time a railroad bridge was built across the Seekonk River extending the line to Providence.

Two other lines later followed the lead of the Boston and Providence Railroad and laid tracks in Old Seekonk. The Providence, Warren and Bristol Railroad chartered in 1850 opened a line in 1855 which traveled south along the river and through present day Riverside. The third railroad to run through the town was opened in 1868, six years after the incorporation of East Providence. The Providence and Worcester Railroad laid tracks from Watchemoket north toward Valley Falls, where this branch tied into the main line running to Worcester.

In spite of their importance the pre-Civil War history of East Providence was not made by mills and railroads but by people. And few, if any, individuals during this period stand out more than Tristam Burges. The son of a cooper in Rochester, Massachusetts, Burges was born in 1770. For most of his childhood and early adult years, he worked in his father's shop and, like many another New England youth, was forced by economic necessity to forego formal schooling almost entirely.

During the first twenty-one years of his life, Burges had accumulated only twelve weeks of classroom time. Still the young man had an inquisitive mind and a deep thirst for knowledge which his family nurtured. His father introduced him to mathematics and his sister taught him to read. When not at work in his father's shop, Burges devoured any reading material he could find. In this way the studious youth had compensated for many of his educational shortcomings.

But Burges had his eyes on college, which required formal preparation. Thus at the age of twenty-one he entered an academy at Wrentham, Massachusetts, where he overcame a speech impediment by long hours of practice in which the birds and the trees in nearby woods served as his audience. As a result of this self-imposed therapy, Burges was chosen valedictorian of his class and would eventually become one of the greatest orators of pre-Civil War America.

After a year in the academy, he entered Brown University in 1793 and once again experienced the academic success which he so passionately sought. He became the best student in his class and was once more chosen valedictorian. Five years of formal education had brought the modest young man from the family of a poor cooper not only knowledge but self confidence—the kind of assurance which, when combined with superior speaking ability and a keen intellect, produces a great lawyer.

In 1799 Burges was admitted to the Rhode Island Bar and quickly established a reputation as one of the outstanding lawyers of the state. It was said that the entire courtroom, not simply the jury, would come to rapt attention whenever he rose to speak. After twenty-five years as a lawyer, Burges was elected to Congress as a representative from Rhode Island. During his two terms in Washington he was more than a match for the skilled southern orators and debaters of the period. "Not a man in the House," one historian has written, "could cope with Rhode Island's representative when once his wrath had been aroused."

After his brief political career, still with many years of life ahead of him, Burges retired to his farm in Old Seekonk (located on Warren Avenue in present day East Providence). Here he died in 1863. Years later the town of East Providence would name one of its streets after this distinguished lawyer and orator. But this largely self taught man would be more appropriately honored when the town opened the Tristam Burges School.

Samuel Bridgham, another prominent Rhode Islander of the pre-Civil War period had even firmer roots than Tristam Burges in the community which was to become East Providence. The youngest son of Dr. Joseph Bridgham, Samuel was born and raised on his father's farm in what is now Rumford. He entered Brown University in 1790 at the age of sixteen, paid his tuition by working as a teacher during vacations, and graduated in 1794 with highest honors. He became a member of the Rhode Island Bar and moved across the Seekonk River to Providence. His political career soon skyrocketed. He served successively as state representative, attorney general, and adjutant-general in the Rhode Island Militia. Finally, when Providence was incorporated as a city in 1832, this native of the Rumford area was elected its first mayor. He remained in that office until his death in 1840.

As politicians and outstanding lawyers, both Bridgham and Tristam Burges were involved from time to time in Rhode Island's protracted legal controversy with Massachusetts over the boundary line between the two states. The dispute began in 1636 when Roger Williams, under the impression that he was in Rhode Island, settled at Seekonk Cove. As one will recall, Massachusetts and Plymouth authorities ordered Williams to leave his initial settlement because, they argued, Rhode Island began on the opposite side of the Seekonk River. The incorporation of East Providence in 1862 vindicated Williams' judgment, but in the decades in between the boundary line between Massachusetts and Rhode Island was a bone of contention.

In the middle of the eighteenth century, the authorities made a major attempt to settle the controversy. In 1741 Rhode Island drew up a claim to land along the eastern shore of Narragansett Bay and other territory adjacent to Mount Hope Bay. The British government appointed commissioners to evaluate this claim. Their ruling was favorable to Rhode Island, and Massachusetts was forced to cede a large tract of territory. As a result of the commissioners' decision in 1747, the towns of Cumberland, Barrington, Bristol, Tiverton and Little Compton which had belonged to Massachusetts became part of Rhode Island.

But in spite of the settlement, the commission failed to determine precisely the location of the boundary line between the two colonies. The point on the eastern side of the Seekonk River and Narragansett Bay where Rhode Island ended and Massachusetts began was unclear. Thus the controversy now revolved around determining this line, with Massachusetts constantly accusing Rhode Island of running the line too far inland. When a commission appointed by Massachusetts did finally agree with Rhode Island on a boundary, the legislature in Boston declared their decision "null and void" and directed that eighty-four stone markers establishing the boundary be toppled.

Further attempts to settle the dispute proved unsuccessful and a new approach to the problem was suggested by Tristam Burges. The people along the disputed boundary, he informed Massachusetts officials in 1848, "will never be satisfied until this line is settled by the *Supreme Court of the United States.*" Four years later in 1852, Massachusetts requested that the Supreme Court establish the exact location of the boundary line of 1747 and settle the controversy once and for all.

Since Massachusetts officials initiated this action, they were undoubtedly confident that the Court would dismiss the claims of Rhode Island and extend the Bay State's boundary line. But when, on the advice of a special commission, the Court made its ruling in 1861, Rhode

Island gained more territory at the expense of her neighboring state. The industrial and agricultural western part of Old Seekonk, along with the important manufacturing town of Pawtucket, were annexed to Rhode Island. A majority of the schools, churches and industries of Old Seekonk as well as the town's center (the old "Ring of the Green") and two-thirds of its population now came under the jurisdiction of Rhode Island.

The new citizens of Rhode Island requested that Governor William Sprague choose a name for their town. On March 1, 1862 he announced his decision and East Providence became part of Rhode Island. As the sun rose on this memorable day in the town's history, a detachment of troops stationed at Fort Hill fired a salute to East Providence. In a short while Governor Sprague appeared at the foot of the Washington Bridge and was greeted by ordinary citizens and state dignitaries. After handshaking and applause he divulged the name of the town. A roar went up from the crowd as individuals began to repeat approvingly, "East Providence, Rhode Island."

People began to parade through the streets, waving flags and signs and creating a festive mood in the community. Many headed for the town hall where East Providence's first town meeting was to be held at 11 o'clock. The meeting was called to order on time and the voters tackled the agenda. A five man town council (no longer called board of selectmen) was elected consisting of Francis Armington, Allen J. Brown, George O. Carpenter, Daniel S. Peck and Austin Gurney. Henry Ide was chosen Town Clerk and Albert C. Gerald was elected Moderator of the town meeting and representative to the Rhode Island General Assembly. Tristam Burges, Esq., son of the famous orator, was selected to be the town's state senator.

In addition to electing the first officials of East Providence, the town meeting passed a number of resolutions which sought the cooperation of Seekonk in settling mutual problems caused by the division of the town. The voters "*Resolved,* That we will seek that the present questions in dispute between ourselves and our former townsmen may be settled in the spirit of kindness and equity; (and) that we will seek 'to do by them as we would be done by'." Dr. Thomas Aspinwall and Tristam Burges, Esq. were directed to deliver this and other resolutions immediately to the residents of "New" Seekonk.

The first town meeting came to a close at twelve o'clock as a second salute to East Providence rang out from Fort Hill. Governor Sprague briefly addressed the citizens and newly elected officials of the town.

Celebrating continued throughout the afternoon and evening and the historic day came to a close with an inaugural ball at the Vue de l'Eau Hotel in Riverside.

Following the festivities of the weekend of March 1st, the approximately 1,850* inhabitants of the town returned to their daily tasks. During the spring and summer of 1862, meetings were called periodically to organize the affairs of the town. East Providence's first budget approved on April 2nd had only three items:

Schools	$ 500
Highways	$1200
Incidentals, including State Tax	$1700

Perhaps the major problem facing the new town was the reorganization of the school system. The separation of Old Seekonk into two towns cut through the old school districts and upset the even distribution of schoolhouses throughout East Providence. Moreover, many of the existing structures were in need of repairs. In the spring of 1862 town officials organized new school districts and launched a campaign to repair old schools and to build new ones. In May $9,500 was appropriated for these purposes.

Soon the Civil War focused the attention of the town officials on national rather than strictly local problems. The war was nearly a year old when East Providence was incorporated in 1862. Already by March 4, 1861 when Abraham Lincoln was inaugurated as President of the United States, southern rebels had seized federal property in the South. A month later the Confederate flag was raised over Fort Sumter in South Carolina. Lincoln's response to this bold act began the hostilities that would continue for four years. On April 15th he requested that state militia men numbering seventy-five thousand form an army to put down the rebellion. Governor Sprague immediately answered Lincoln's call, and on April 20th General Burnside (the only New England general in the Civil War) led the 1st Regiment of the Rhode Island Detached

**Several writers have used the figure 1,250 for the population of East Providence in 1862, but this is not accurate. Since the census of 1865 gave the town a population of 2,172, it is hardly likely that it would have increased by over 900 (or nearly 70%) in three years – war years at that! After the division in 1862 the population of Seekonk was about 800.*

Militia from Providence to Washington.

During the first year of hostilities the war went badly for the North. Faced with a worsening military position and growing opposition to his conduct of the war, Lincoln made a second appeal for 300,000 men in July 1862. States were assigned quotas which they apportioned out to towns and cities which held the responsibility for enlisting volunteers and/or draftees.

At this time East Providence appropriated funds for soldiers and the machinery to recruit them was set in motion. Money was put aside for a recruiting office and for an advertising campaign to attract volunteers. A committee of four citizens, representing both the northern and southern regions of the town, was established to implement the recruitment drive. To entice volunteers, a bounty was offered and money was also voted for the support of the families of those who enlisted in the army. Each family would receive four dollars per week as long as the head of the household was in the service.

In addition to supplying soldiers, the community supported the northern cause in other ways. Like most Rhode Island towns, East Providence participated in relief work which had as its goal the spiritual and physical well-being of the Union troops. National organizations such as the Sanitary and Christian Commissioners and local groups like the Providence Association for the Relief of Volunteers supplied the army with items ranging from Bibles, towels and underwear to bandages, soap, and razor blades. In East Providence the Soldiers Aid Society met from time to time in the town hall. But much of the town's relief work was channeled through organizations in Providence. To the Sanitary Commission alone, Providence contributed over $18,000 in cash (and perhaps as much in goods) and a portion of this money doubtless came from the people of East Providence.

By 1863 the Union Army needed manpower more than money and materiel. Only 80,000 recruits had responded to Lincoln's call of the previous year. To remedy this situation Congress passed a new draft law in March 1863. Unfortunately, this law created as many problems as it solved. A draftee could be exempted from service by supplying a substitute or by paying $300. Consequently, protests against this undemocratic arrangement flared. In New York full scale rioting broke out as mobs set fires and attacked free blacks. Union soldiers were sent to the city to suppress this rebellion behind the lines.

The people of East Providence also expressed their discontent with the new draft law, although they chose peaceful means. In June 1863 a town meeting was called to make arrangements to fill the town's quota of recruits. State Senator Francis Armington presented a resolution, on behalf of many people in the community, protesting the exemption provision of the draft law: "Whereas the citizens of this town feel that the burden should be born (sic) equally on the rich and poor therefore Resolved that Francis Armington, James Barney and T. F. Neville be a committee to wait on his excellency the Governor and request him to convene the General Assembly in special session that acts may be passed in relation to the same." Of course, the draft came under federal not state jurisdiction, and neither Lincoln nor Congress changed the law measurably for the remainder of the war.

While the draft was creating a controversy, Rhode Island received a mild war scare. The small Confederate navy had been successfully preying on trading vessels sailing to and from northern harbors. In June 1863 a rebel ship made a daring move into the harbor at Portland, Maine, with guns sending cannon balls at docked vessels and toward the shore. Although the Confederate ship was captured, Rhode Islanders were alarmed because Narragansett Bay made them extremely vulnerable to the hit and run tactics of the Confederate navy. The area was a doubly inviting target for the rebels because at the beginning of the war Federal officials had shifted the Naval Academy at Annapolis to Newport. Thus a successful Confederate naval attack on the Narragansett Bay area would provide the rebels with symbolic and real victories.

Shortly after the raid on Portland, state officials began to make preparations to avert a similar occurrence in Rhode Island. In June 1863 Governor James Y. Smith sent a letter to President Lincoln informing him that "Great anxiety is felt here on account of the unprotected condition of Narragansett Bay. There is nothing to prevent a rebel incursion through 'West Passage,' exposing to destruction this city (Providence), Fall River and other towns on the Bay." It was Smith's understanding that the War Department had plans for an earthwork fortification on the Bay. The Governor requested these plans along with money and the authority to begin construction and to initiate a program of inspecting all ships sailing on the Bay.

Secretary of War Edward Stanton wrote back at once giving Lincoln's sanction to the project and making available the blueprints, and an engineer from his department. A breastwork was erected and a camp, named after the governor, was laid out nearby where a battery of Rhode Island militia was stationed.

Within two weeks of Governor Smith's letter to Lincoln, the tide of the war turned in favor of the Union army, diminishing the threat of a naval raid on Rhode Island. During the first three days of July 1863, the greatest battle of the war was fought at Gettysburg in Pennsylvania. General Robert E. Lee was soundly defeated by the Union army. His ambitious plan to bring the war into the heart of the North was now dead and, with it, 28,000 of his soldiers. The following day, July 4, General Ulysses S. Grant captured Vicksburg, "the Gibraltar of the Mississippi." The South would never recover from these major setbacks.

The war dragged on until the spring of 1865 and finally in April Lee surrendered to Grant at Appamattox. Soon church bells announced the end of hostilities and the beginning of a time for reflection and taking stock. More than 24,000 Rhode Islanders fought for the Union cause and many of these saw their homes and relatives for the last time when they marched off to battle.

But they had not died in vain. The Union was preserved and along the way slavery, always a secondary issue in Lincoln's mind, was abolished. Peace ushered in a fifty year period of tremendous growth marked by the interplay of industrialization, urbanization and immigration from which 'the face of modern America' emerged. East Providence shared in this expansion and between 1865 and the First World War the outlines of the contemporary city became visible.

V
Watchemoket, Rumford and Phillipsdale, 1865-1917

In terms of pure numbers, the growth of East Providence during the period from 1865 to American entry in World War I was remarkable. From a population of less than 2,200 in 1865, the town swelled to over 4,300 in 1875, a growth rate of almost 100 percent in ten years. Fortunately for East Providence officials, this surge receded somewhat after 1875, but the population continued to expand each decade (until the Depression) by from 25 to 50 percent.

In 1885, for example, the town numbered over 6,800 residents. Ten years later, this figure had climbed to 10,170, and by 1905 nearly 14,000 people made East Providence their home. Finally in 1915, the census recorded 18,584 inhabitants or ten times as many people (1,850) as had lived in the town fifty-three years earlier when East Providence was incorporated. This amounted to an astounding growth rate of 1000 percent between 1862 and 1915.

The town increased not only in numbers but in complexity and diversity. The once relatively homogeneous "old stock" Protestant population (English, Scottish, Scots-Irish, German and Swedish) gradually evolved into an ethnic mixture as Irish, Portuguese, Italian and French Canadian Catholics (and a sprinkling of Jews and blacks) made their way to the eastern shore of the Seekonk River. The town itself was as diverse as the people who comprised its population. Four distinct villages emerged in the decades after the Civil War.

From the foot of Washington Bridge and extending eastward lay the town's new political, communal and population center, still referred to by its Indian name, Watchemoket. In the area of the old "Ring of the Green" there emerged a mill village which came to be called Rumford. In the northwest corner of the town another manufacturing community Phillipsdale – developed. Finally, the small fishing and farming area in the southern part of the town became a fashionable summer resort called Riverside.

Because of their diversity in historical development, it is necessary to analyze each village independently. Indeed, so different (and important) was the experience of Riverside that a separate chapter will be devoted to its history between 1865 and World War I. Of the other areas of East Providence, Watchemoket was by far the most important. Thus it is with its story that we begin.

Watchemoket

In the decades preceding the Civil War, Watchmoket Point was little more than a farming and fishing area with perhaps a few hundred residents. But because of its location it was destined to become, in the post war years, the hub of the new town of East Providence.

In the first place, Watchemoket was situated directly across from the thriving city of Providence and thus benefited from the expansion

Modern-day Watchemoket Square

An early postcard view of Watchemoket Square

of that community. More important, two bridges across the Seekonk gave easy access to Watchemoket. By the 1860's tolls were no longer being charged to cross the Washington and Central Bridges, giving a further stimulus to the growth of Watchemoket. Furthermore, two new structures were built at the site of the old bridges to accommodate the expanding traffic between Providence and East Providence. In 1869 the famous Red Bridge was completed, and in 1885 a new Washington Bridge was opened.

Two railroad trestles crossed the Seekonk, providing transportation facilities required for the development of industry. Perhaps even more crucial, the river itself, flowing into Narragansett Bay which opened on the Atlantic Ocean, offered a natural water route for cargo ships. Moreover, because of its location Watchemoket became not only a rail and water crossroads but a highway crossroads as well. In addition to the heavily traveled Boston Post Road running from Pawtucket Avenue to the Washington Bridge, highways to Taunton (Route 44), Fall River (Route 6) and to Barrington, Warren and Bristol all intersected at Watchemoket.

The transformation of the village from a sleepy fishing and farming area to the vital core of a bustling town came swiftly on the heels of the incorporation of East Providence in 1862. Perhaps the first businesses to come to Watchemoket were inns built to service the large numbers of

A postcard view of Red Bridge in Providence at the turn of the century

The new Washington Bridge opened in 1931 and carried travelers into a developing East Providence. This view is from Fort Hill.

people who traveled daily through the area. Service industries of this kind were quickly followed by other businesses and Watchemoket Square began to take shape.

The Ingraham family became the chief commercial developers of the area. Much of Watchemoket's farming land belonged to them and in the 1860's they initiated construction of the first substantial structure at the busy intersection. The Ingraham Building greeted the endless stream of travelers crossing the Washington Bridge and gave them a good first impression of East Providence. The building was constructed of steel and red brick and stood two stories high. It extended for nearly 150 feet along the Fall River Road (present day Warren Avenue) and housed stores and offices on the first floor and a hall and apartments on the second. A huge doorway in the center of the building opened on a ramp which led to the second floor hall. When the Wild West Show came to East Providence (we must remember that this was the heyday of Buffalo Bill and other traveling cowboy and Indian groups who introduced the "wild" West to the "civilized" East), wagons, horses and other animals mounted the ramp to reach the hall where the show was performed.

The Town of East Providence also made use of the Ingraham Building. Since the population center of the community had shifted toward Watchemoket, the old town hall in Rumford was too far away to serve many of the town's residents. Therefore, a mini town hall opened in the Ingraham Building where one could pay taxes, register deeds or take out a marriage license. A post office and the Watchemoket Fire District Water Company also occupied space in the Ingraham Building.

The residents of Watchemoket also had their own library by the early 1870's. In 1871 a group of women met in Lyceum Hall at Watchemoket Square and formed a library association. Books were collected and small fees were charged for their use. At first the organizers called themselves the Ladies Library Association, but in 1885 they changed this name to the Watchemoket Free Public Library. By the 1880's this second library to be established in East Providence contained over 1,700 volumes which were circulated at no charge.

The early faith of the Ingraham family in the future of Watchemoket proved to be well placed. As early as the mid-1880's the village had become the most populated area in East Providence, and by 1890 it held the town's central business district. Numerous docks and piers extended into the Seekonk River. The largest of these – the Wilkesbarre

The Wilkesbarre Pier on the Seekonk handled the heaviest industrial traffic in the area in the late 19th century.

Pier – stretched for about a thousand feet along the shore and was a major receiving and shipping point for the lucrative coal business of the Providence and Worcester Railroad. In 1880 alone, 473 cargoes were unloaded at the pier and over 256,000 tons of coal were transported by rail from East Providence to points all over New England.

Not far from the Wilkesbarre Pier stood a diversified business and manufacturing district. Two large oyster houses packed and shipped that salt water delicacy to locations for miles around. Also on the shore at Watchemoket was the Providence Dry Dock and Marine Railway Company which operated a floating dock. On nearby Valley Street was located the Huntington Maple Syrup and Refinery which bottled maple syrup, sugar cane and honey and shipped these products around the country.

An equally important industry was the Narragansett Milling Company which built a large mill at Watchemoket in 1894. This company received grain from the "breadbasket states" of the midwest, processed it into usable form and shipped it to towns in the southern New England area. Two other noteworthy businesses employing many hands at

The Oyster House by the Washington Bridge was one of the centers for packing and shipping this Rhode Island delicacy.

Watchemoket were The Eastern Bolt and Nut Company and the Bullard Automatic Wrench Company. In addition, a number of smaller manufacturing and business concerns such as repair shops, markets and dry-goods stores flourished in the area.

Already the commercial and population center of East Providence by the mid-1880's, Watchemoket next became the political center as well. It no longer made sense to hold town meetings in the old town hall in Rumford, several miles away from the heart of the community. Nor did it seem appropriate that the people of the burgeoning village of Watchemoket had only a mini-town hall in the Ingraham Building to serve them. What East Providence needed was a new town hall which in size and appearance accurately reflected the prosperity and growth of the town, lent it an air of governmental respectability and encouraged civic pride.

Watchemoket was the logical location for the new structure. A lot was purchased on Taunton Avenue for $11,500 and in 1888 $35,000 was appropriated for the new town hall. The attractive two story brick building, with well manicured grounds surrounding it, was opened in 1889. The structure was built to provide office space on the first floor, and a hall for public meetings and entertainment on the second. In 1890 the Watchemoket Free Library became one of the first public service institutions to move into the new building.

That same year the East Providence Police Department opened its headquarters on one side of the town hall. For years the department had contained only five constables under the supervision of the town council which appointed them. In 1887 Charles E. Pierce was named the first Chief of Police in charge of five men who patrolled three districts: Watchemoket, Riverside and Phillipsdale. The men made their rounds on horseback and worked about eleven hours a day for which they received approximately $1,200 a year.

In the late nineteenth century the department averaged about 200 arrests per year, usually for misdemeanors. A police report for one year during the period reveals that crime in the rapidly expanding community was of a relatively minor and non-violent nature. The 230 men and 13 women arrested in 1874-75 were charged with the following offenses:

> drunk, 78; assault, 7; larceny, 14; exposure of person, 3; bathing against ordinance, 6; of doubtful reputation, 4; disorderly conduct, 23; cruelty to animals, 3; maintaining a grog shop, 2; illegal sale of liquors, 7; shop open after hours, 1; revelling, 53; keeping liquor nuisance, 5; keeping liquor for sale, 6; recreation on Sunday, 2; shops open on Sunday, 26; breaking and entering in the night-time, 1; obtaining money on false pretenses, 1.

Many of these breaches of the law occurred during the summer in the Riverside area when thousands of people came each weekend to the numerous campsites, beaches and shore dinner halls.

Even after the turn of the century, the East Providence Police Department remained small, consisting of the chief, two sergeants and a handful (between 6 and 10) of patrolmen. But at least the department had full time, paid officers. The same could not be said of the fire department which depended totally upon volunteers until 1911.

Seven volunteer fire companies were spread out across East Providence from Riverside to Phillipsdale and Rumford. The most important of these was the Watchemoket Fire Company No. 1, located next to the police station on Taunton Avenue. On the sound of an alarm, volunteers dropped whatever they were doing and raced on foot to the station where firefighting equipment was stored. Motorized vehicles were not introduced until 1911 and before that apparatus were drawn by hand.

As bystanders identified the location of the fire, the panting and leg weary volunteers pulled and pushed their vehicle as fast as they could, occasionally tripping in a pothole or on a stone (most streets were not paved at this time). Excited children and curious adults hurried behind the firefighters, giving the scene something of a holiday atmosphere. If the volunteers were fortunate, they found a passing horse and wagon, hitched their apparatus to it and arrived at the site of the fire still left with sufficient energy to battle the blaze effectively. Sometimes, especially in the Watchemoket area, a fire fighting wagon was attached to the rear of an electric street car and drawn to the burning building.

With all the physical exertion involved in answering a call, false alarms became a particularly exasperating problem. Not pranksters but the primitive alarm system of the department proved to be the main culprit. Church bells were first used to summon the volunteers, but the Watchemoket firemen requested that a bell be placed in their station. "This seems to us," they informed the town council, "far better and safer than (depending) on the church bell which is often used for other purposes thereby tending to confusion and at the same time not as convenient to the fire department." Soon a bell was placed in the newly constructed town hall which sounded the alarm for the Watchemoket Fire Company. Shortly after this Watchemoket became the first district in the town to have alarm boxes, and this innovation was followed by the hiring of the first full time firemen in the years before World War I.

Like the police and fire departments, the school system of East Providence expanded and modernized in the late nineteenth and early twentieth century. The tremendous growth in the town's population required new and larger schools, especially in the Watchemoket area where many new residents settled. Since 1800 East Providence (then Old Rehoboth) had been divided into school districts run by district

Watchemoket Square as it appeared in the early part of the 20th century

trustees. These groups of local citizens called meetings, raised taxes, hired teachers and in general governed the affairs of the local school district. The district system was not equitable because the wealthier and more populous areas in the town could raise more money and thus provide better educational facilities than the poorer, thinly populated, outlying districts. In 1877 this system was abolished and it was voted "That the town provide schools without reference to its division into school districts."

Throughout the late nineteenth century school construction was required to keep pace with an expanding population. By the early 1870's evening schools were opened in Watchemoket and Rumford to serve working people who wanted to continue their education. The school committee reported in 1876 that the town's foreign immigrants also found the evening schools valuable and "gladly availed themselves of this opportunity to acquire the language and modes of expression of our country." Other schools, that by now would have served several generations of East Providence residents, were opened during this period, some of which bore the names of former school superintendents or chairmen of the school committee: the Grove Avenue School (1876), the A. P. Hoyt Grammar School (1891), the William B. Ellis Primary School (1897) and the George S. Dean School (1905).

One measure of the tremendous growth of the school system may be seen in the town's appropriations for education. From $500 in 1862, the cost of maintaining East Providence's schools rose to $8,100 by 1875 and to $23,624 by 1889. These figures would have been considerably higher except for the fact that it was not until 1894 that a state law was passed requiring towns to furnish textbooks and supplies to students. Up until that year parents purchased this material.

An appointed committee ran the school system, and until 1903 they chose one of their members to serve as superintendent. Among the school committee's chief responsibilities was the hiring of teachers, not always an easy task. Tenure was unheard of at that time and pay was rather low. The thirty-eight teachers in the East Providence School System in 1889, for example, collected weekly salaries ranging from $15 for grammar school principals (who also taught) to $8 and $7 for pri-

At the turn of the century, Union Primary School in Rumford schooled Phillipsdale youth who wanted an education beyond the fourth grade. It was a three mile journey.

The old wooden East Providence High School on Grove Avenue, as it appears on diplomas: it achieved scholastic recognition in 1894 when its graduates were admitted to Brown University "without further examination."

mary school teachers. It is little wonder, then, that the school committee lamented periodically that many teachers viewed their occupation "as a stepping stone to higher position and better remuneration."

The highest paid position in the school system belonged, in 1889, to J. Irwin Chaffee, the first principal of East Providence High School, who received $30 a week. As early as 1867 the school committee had suggested "that the best interests of the town would be promoted by making provision for a high school." But it was not until 1884 that a room was set aside at the Mauran Avenue School for the high school. Chaffee served as both principal and teacher to the first class of 28 students. At the time he was a twenty-three year old graduate of Brown University who two years earlier, while still a student in college, had been appointed principal of the Grove Avenue Grammar School. He taught and administered the high school for six years.

During that time enrollment more than doubled and in 1888 the town voted to move the high school to more spacious quarters at the Grove Avenue School, where it would remain for nearly two decades. The school was designed primarily to prepare students for college. In their *Annual Report of 1892,* the school committee expressed its desire "to place it (the high school) in line with its nearest competition, the Providence (Classical) High School, a diploma from which guarantees to the pupil holding it, entrance into Brown University without further examination." By 1894 the school committee's goal had been achieved as graduates of East Providence High School were no longer required to take entrance examinations for Brown but were admitted solely on the recommendation of the principal.

In future years changes were needed to maintain the respected reputation of the high school, and the quality of the school system in general. By 1899 over 2,400 children were enrolled in East Providence schools, requiring a budget of $37,000. As the population of the town increased, enrollment swelled. In the fast growing Watchemoket area, the central school district students could no longer be accommodated in existing schools, which resulted in the opening of makeshift classrooms in nearby commercial buildings. "The overflow of grammar pupils in the Watchemoket District," the School Committee noted in its *Annual Report for 1907,* "was relieved by rooms hired outside – one in the Tobin Block – one in the Leslie Block. At mid-year the hall of the A. P. Hoyt School was fitted with ten foot partitions and four emergency recitation rooms provided."

The high school experienced similar growing pains. Beginning in 1901, and each year for nearly a decade thereafter, the school committee recommended the construction of a new high school. It no longer seemed realistic for the growing number of high schoolers to share the Grove Avenue building with grammar school students. But the people of East Providence voted in their financial town meeting of 1901 simply to build an addition to the Grove Avenue School and not to construct a new high school.

In spite of the added space students still had to be taught in the basement of the school where, the school committee reported, "it was so dark that electric lights were used every day and ventilation was poor." Thus school system personnel continued to push for a new building and in 1908, after refusing to appropriate town money, the voters approved a bond issue. East Providence officials were directed to request authority from the General Assembly for the town to issue $100,000 in bonds to purchase land, build and equip a new high school, and to construct any other school buildings that were deemed necessary.

As workmen proceeded with the new structure on Taunton Avenue, high school classes were held in the Leslie Building and in the town hall. The District Court Room, the firemen's parlors and even the school superintendent's office were transformed into algebra, Latin, English and history classrooms. The long-awaited high school was finally completed in 1910. An open house was held and the citizens of East Providence filed through the building which contained the latest equipment in its laboratories and classrooms. Unfortunately, the school was designed for a maximum enrollment of 400, and the surge of students in the pre-World War I years once again confronted school officials with the reality of crowded conditions. As early as 1912, school officials were forced to make the lunchroom into a classroom.

As town officials had recognized for some time, overcrowding and other problems created by the expansion of the school system required a full time, paid administrator. By the time East Providence High School opened in 1910, the school system was already under the leadership of its second professional administrator. In 1903 the old practice of electing a member of the school committee to serve as superintendent was ended and Allen P. Keith took over administrative leadership of the school system. He was succeeded in 1910 by James R. D. Oldham, who would remain in the position for thirty-four years.

East Providence officials were faced not only with growing numbers of students but also with a school population, particularly in the Watchemoket area, that was increasingly diverse in ethnic composition. The Irish, who comprised the single largest ethnic group in East Providence until very recently, began their migration to the town before the Civil War. East Providence's post-war growth created many jobs and large numbers of Irish left Providence, where they had first settled after arriving in America, for the town on the opposite side of the Seekonk River. At first these Catholic residents of East Providence had to journey back across the Washington Bridge or to St. Joseph's Church in Pawtucket to attend Sunday mass. But by the late 1870's their numbers had grown sufficiently for the diocese to provide them with their own church. In 1880 the Church of the Sacred Heart, the first Catholic church in East

Providence, was opened on Taunton Avenue in the center of Watchemoket with the Reverend Francis O'Reilly as its pastor.

Almost simultaneous with the founding of the Church of the Sacred Heart, the people who constitute the largest ethnic group in contemporary East Providence began making their way to the town. Small groups of Portuguese settled in the town in the 1880's and 1890's. During these decades a large Portuguese community was developing in the Fox Point section of Providence just across the Washington Bridge. East Providence's Portuguese community began as an offshoot of the Fox Point settlement but it soon demonstrated evidence it would eclipse the earlier settlement in size.

Beginning around 1900 and continuing until the onset of the Depression in 1930, large numbers of Portuguese from Providence, Fall River, New Bedford and Portugal itself (primarily the Azores Islands) settled in East Providence. By 1905 there were over 400 Portuguese in the town, the third highest total in the State of Rhode Island. Providence and Bristol contained more Portuguese at that time, but by the 1930's East Providence would surpass these two and contain the largest (5,500) Portuguese community in the State.

The Portuguese were heavily concentrated in the Watchemoket area with others living primarily in Rumford. Like their countrymen in Providence, Fall River and New Bedford, the Portuguese of East Providence were employed for the most part in mills and factories. The community had strong ties to Providence since relatives and friends lived in Fox Point. In addition, Providence contained the closest Portuguese church, around which much of the Old World culture revolved.

Therefore, the establishment of a Portuguese church in East Providence was an historic event, symbolizing the maturity and independence of the more recent immigrant community. In 1914 Bishop Matthew Harkins assigned the Reverend Jose P. Lopes the task of conducting a census of the Portuguese in East Providence preliminary to establishing a parish. Funds were raised throughout the year and in 1915 Saint Francis Xavier Church – the third Catholic Church in East Providence, the second being Saint Brendan's in Riverside – became the religious and cultural focal point of the Portuguese community. Soon religious feasts were celebrated regularly and processions marched through the streets of East Providence, adding a new cultural dimension to the town.

The Portuguese, like other ethnic groups, were drawn to East Providence primarily by the lure of jobs. Many employment opportunities were available in the Watchemoket area where numerous immigrants settled. But just as important was the heavy demand for workers which the booming mill villages of Rumford and Phillipsdale created.

Rumford

For some time after the incorporation of the town in 1862, the area around the old "Ring of the Green" was referred to as East Providence Center. The official town hall was located here (until 1889) as were several important churches. Moreover, the village was the population center of East Providence, containing many farms and a number of mills along the Ten Mile River.

Yet forces were at work which would rob the area of its former importance and prestige and transform the farmland surrounding the site of the more than two hundred year old "Ring of the Green" into a thriving mill village. Where the glistening white Newman Congregational Church had stood as the preeminent landmark, expressing the religious ideals behind the settlement of the area, a red and white water tower, built in the shape of a baking powder can and belonging to the Rum-

The site of the old town hall, demolished in 1957, is marked by this plaque located near the Rumford Library.

An old postcard view of Providence from Fort Hill, when masted schooners and the Fall River line boats plied the Seekonk

The Fort Hill site marker, inscribed by the Bicentennial Committee in 1975, marks the location of a fort during the Revolutionary War.

A water tower in the shape of a Rumford Baking Powder can was a hallmark in the area's development as an industrial center.

ford Chemical Works, would come to represent the new way of life in the oldest section of East Providence. The transformation of the village was as complete as these opposing pieces of architecture suggest.

The meteoric rise of Watchemoket as the new center of town drained East Providence Center not only of many of its people, but also of much of its identity and prominence as well. The relative decline of the village in importance between 1865 and World War I was reflected in the fate of the old town hall. For a number of years after incorporation it remained the civic center of East Providence. But by 1880 it was in need of repair and the bulk of the population, no longer living in its shadow, was in favor of constructing a new building in Watchemoket, the new center of town. When the new town hall was opened in 1889, the old structure remained standing and was used by various civic groups. The Center Volunteer Fire Company, for example, used the building as its fire station. When just prior to World War I this group all but ceased to exist, the town hall became a target for vandals who broke its windows, requiring officials to board up the historic old building. At just about this time, construction was begun on the Rumford Chemical Work's tower nearby. This structure was completed in 1919, culminating more than half a century of growth for the internationally known company, growth which dramatically altered the face of East Providence Center.

The Rumford Chemical Works was founded by George F. Wilson and came to East Providence (then Old Seekonk) in 1857. Wilson was born on his father's farm in Uxbridge, Massachusetts in 1818. He was fortunate enough to attend school until the age of seventeen, and then was apprenticed to learn the wool sorting trade by day which allowed him to study on his own at night.

Three years later he completed his apprenticeship not only with a thorough knowledge of the wool business but also with drawings he had made of all the machines in the mill. A sharp, inquisitive intellect and a determination to succeed, when combined with this valuable experience and with a little more formal education thrown in for good measure, destined Wilson for a successful business career.

In 1838 he enrolled at an academy in Shelburne Falls, Massachusetts and after graduation served as a teacher in the school. Wilson next decided to journey to Chicago where he and his wife founded and ran the Chicago Academy for four years. He returned to the East in 1848 and for the next six years worked for several companies in the Providence area. Finally, in 1855, he formed a partnership with Professor E. N. Horsford of Harvard University for "building up a chemical manufacturing establishment of respectability and permanency, such as shall be an honor to ourselves and our children, and a credit to the community in which it is located, and which shall afford us a means of reasonable support."

The old town hall that served Rumford until 1889 (see plaque, p. 96)

The Pomham Light (above) and the grounds of the Pomham Club in Riverside, like the Crescent Park merry-go-round (right), were the sites of many excursions. The carousel is now on the National Historic Register.

Land that originally belonged to Ellery Wilson is, today, the Wannamoisett Golf Club.

A postcard scene of the Squantum Club and Boyden Heights Park

The bust of Benjamin Thompson (Count Rumford) on the grounds of the Rumford Library: he endowed the Harvard professorship whose occupant, Dr. Horsford, brought new industrial development — and a new name — to the area.

In 1857 the George F. Wilson Company was moved from Providence to East Providence and its name was changed to the Rumford Chemical Works. The new name was supplied by Professor Horsford who held the Rumford Chair of the Application of Science to the Useful Arts. This Harvard professorship had been endowed by Benjamin Thompson, a physicist who after serving the Duke of Bavaria returned to America and called himself Count Rumford. Thompson had taken the name from a town – Rumford, New Hampshire – where he had taught school. Once Wilson and Horsford's company expanded and their mill village took shape, East Providence Center would come to be known as Rumford.

The two partners complemented each other: one contributed practical skills while his opposite number devoted his time to theory. The success of Rumford Chemical was built upon Wilson's business sense and knowledge of machinery and Horsford's understanding of chemistry. At first the company manufactured an entire line of chemical products used in printing and dyeing. Quite early, though, Wilson and Horsford decided to concentrate on a compound of pulverulent acid phosphate which was called Horsford's Cream of Tartar. Most of this product was used in Horsford's Baking Powder and Rumford Yeast Powder. In addition the two partners manufactured a medicinal product called Horsford's Acid Phosphate. All of these products became common in households throughout the country, and Rumford came to be called "the kitchen capital of the world." Even today Rumford Baking Powder, now being produced in Indiana, can be found in many if not most homes.

Not only did the company prosper, but so did Wilson's standing in the community. Until 1861 he was a resident of Providence and, between getting his business off the ground and patenting inventions, he managed to serve an extended tenure on the school committee and two terms in the General Assembly. He moved to East Providence in 1861 and was soon called into public service. He won four elections to the school committee and one to the town council.

Wilson had long envisioned establishing more than a factory. Perhaps one reason why he moved his company to East Providence was because the large tracts of farming land in the old "Ring of the Green" area offered him an opportunity to found a self-sufficient mill village. He bought much of the acreage which had belonged to the original homesteads of Old Rehoboth and established a company farm, pasturage and dairy. When work was slack in the Chemical Factory employees were kept busy in the fields or at the dairy. By 1872, 325 acres of land were being farmed and 175 acres served as pasture land.

Numerous horses and oxen performed the heavy work on the farm and 150 hogs and a herd of livestock supplied the meat needs of the employees. At the beginning of 1872 Rumford officials predicted that 25,000 pounds of pork and 18,000 pounds of beef would be handled in the company's slaughterhouse. At the same time the dairy house processed butter, cheese and milk from a herd of company cows. All of the goods produced on the farm were sold to employees in the company store.

In addition, workers rented company houses and had the use of a community building which Wilson erected for them on Greewood Avenue. Small clusters of company housing were scattered along the streets surrounding the plant. At the end of Newman Avenue, for example, a number of tenements that were formerly part of the Central Mills complex housed Rumford Chemical Works employees. Other company houses, most of which are still standing, were built on North Broadway.

The old Washington Bridge across the Seekonk, built in 1793 by John Brown, was the first covered drawbridge in America *(see p. 64)**. Note Fort Hill to the right.*

The new Washington Bridge was built in 1931 to keep pace with growth and industrial development *(see also p. 63)**.*

A network of bridges spanned the Seekonk by the time this early 20th century post-card photograph was taken.

An oil painting of the Watchemoket train depot shows an older, quieter time. (Note touring car.)

Dating back to the 17th century, the old "house that never moved" has survived changing boundaries and place names. It is located on the corner of Wilson and Roger Williams Avenues.

As early as the mid-1870's the Rumford Chemical Works claimed ownership of between one-half and two-thirds of the area bounded by Centre Street on the south, the Pawtucket city line on the north, the Massachusetts state line on the east and the Seekonk River on the west. At this time the total assets of the company were valued at over $500,000. Like many successful late nineteenth century entrepreneurs, Wilson donated a portion of his profits to educational institutions and charitable causes. He bequeathed $50,000 to Dartmouth College for the construction of a library and donated twice that amount to Brown University for a laboratory.

Ellery Wilson, who succeeded his father as president of the company, also aided the founding of two churches in Rumford. In the years after the Civil War a number of Irish Catholics from Providence and Pawtucket came to live and work in the village. These Catholic inhabitants of Rumford were officially part of St. Joseph's parish in Pawtucket, but mass was said for them in a private residence at the corner of Newport and Roger Williams Avenues. In 1886 Rumford was designated as a mission of the Church of the Sacred Heart in Watchemoket. Two years later, Bishop Harkins approved plans for the construction of a church in Rumford.

The parishioners launched a subscription drive and raised nearly $1,000. Ellery Wilson donated an additional $500 and a parcel of land for the church. Each evening for several weeks in the fall of 1888, the Catholic men of Rumford, after a full day of work, met at the construction site and labored until dark to erect the basement of the church. When their task was completed, a private contractor began work on the church itself. In the spring of 1890 Bishop Harkins dedicated the original building of St. Margaret's Church.

Shortly after the new church opened a large number of Swedes settled alongside the Irish and the more established Anglo-Saxon community in Rumford. The Swedes were heavily concentrated in the Ferris Avenue area, and they found employment opportunities either at the Rumford Chemical Works or in Phillipsdale. In 1895 Ellery Wilson donated a piece of land on Ferris Avenue for the establishment of a Swedish mission which later became the Good Shepherd Lutheran Church.

By 1890 the Rumford Chemical Works had conferred a new identity on the old town center. The numerous workers who populated the mill village referred to themselves as Rumford people, since most aspects of their lives revolved around the Chemical Company. When in 1889 the new town hall opened in Watchemoket, the term East Providence Center dropped from usage and was permanently replaced by the name Rumford.

The village numbered between six and seven hundred inhabitants, more than half of whom were in the employ of the chemical works. Each morning the company whistle, which was also used to alert the Rumford Volunteer Fire Company, announced the beginning of a new work day at the efficiently run mill complex. After a long week of hard work, perhaps many Rumford families spent part of their weekend at nearby Hunts' Mills where a dance hall and amusements were now located in the midst of the beautiful scenery.

Rumford continued to prosper up to and beyond World War I. Gradually in the late nineteenth century and continuing into the early twentieth century, Rumford Chemical officials divided, plotted and sold parts of the company's extensive real estate. (Major residential development of the area, however, would not occur until the 1930's and 1940's.) Throughout the years the company's baking powder carried the name Rumford far and wide. Wilson and Horsford were now long dead, but their contributions to the growth of Rumford were commem-

The Newman Church

The Willett Stone honors an Old Rehoboth citizen who became the first mayor of New York in 1665 (see p. 29).

An early postcard view of the East Providence Town Hall, when the building also housed the Fire Department and the Library

A view of City Hall from Purchase Street, with the United States and Bicentennial flags flying.

Unknown to many present-day residents is the fact that an amusement center was located at Hunts' Mills until the 1920's. In this postcard scene, dated 1906, the sign over the center building reads "Vaudeville."

orated when two avenues running through the village were named in their honor.

Beginning in 1919, visitors traveling on Wilson Avenue near North Broadway would find staring down at them one of the tallest structures in East Providence, a unique 165-foot water tower. It was a monument to the inventiveness and business ability of the two men who founded the company that radically changed East Providence's old town center.

Phillipsdale

Contemporary with the development of Rumford village, and only a mile or two to the west of it, another flourishing mill complex came into existence. The area bordering on Seekonk Cove (later Omega Pond), it will be recalled, was the site of Roger Williams' settlement, and in the early history of Old Rehoboth it became a commercial area with wharves and shops. Before the Civil War, manufacturers moved into the village. The Omega Mills, for example, lodged in the Old Stone House on Roger Williams Avenue in East Providence, became an important manufacturer of cotton cloth. As in Rumford, the area took on the name of its most important company and came to be known as Omega Village, numbering between two and three hundred people by 1870.

About this time the mill and the workers' houses, which were located on both sides of the railroad bridge on Roger Williams Avenue, were purchased by the Rumford Chemical Works. The village was renamed Clyde, and the mill manufactured spring rings, spindles and other items used in the textile industry.

Sometime during the post-Civil War years another company, the Richmond Paper Mill, moved to the Omega Pond area; but this section of Roger Williams Avenue remained an obscure backwater of East Providence down through the early 1890's. "The place was regarded as part of the ragged edge of Rumford," the *Providence Journal* observed later, "and so unimportant as to be unworthy of a distinctive name."

But when Eugene Phillips decided to move his copper mill to the edge of Omega Pond, a new chapter in the history of the village began. A native of Scituate, Rhode Island, Phillips started his wire business in an old, run-down barn on Chestnut Street in Providence in 1870 when he was only 27 years old. The young man had hit upon such a solid idea for a business that he was soon to outgrow these quarters. Phillips

The mill homes on Roger Williams Avenue in Phillipsdale

An old postard view of Hunts' Mills

The Hunts' homestead at the old mill site, with the modern water department sign visible

A turn-of-the-century photograph of Omega Pond and Clyde's Mills, with the Cove Factory on the right

bought copper wire, covered it with insulation and sold it to others. The demand for this product was just beginning in the early 1870's. In a few years telephones would spread across the country and, somewhat later, electric streetcars and streetlights would create a major market for insulated wire.

For the first few years, however, Phillips worked by himself in his Providence barn and managed to insulate about fifty pounds of wire a day. He began to receive more orders, and in 1873 he sold his barn and bought a part of a larger building in South Providence. Phillips' business and work force increased throughout the 1870's and by the end of the decade he was sponsoring a company clambake for his workers and customers at Rhodes on the Pawtuxet.

By 1880 the copper business had taken over the entire building in South Providence, but Phillips still needed more space and workers to meet the demand for his product. He constructed a large brick building on the same site and incorporated his company as the American Electrical Works. In 1889 another copper mill was opened in Canada and incorporated as the Eugene F. Phillips Electrical Works, Ltd. of Montreal.

For the future history of the Omega Pond area in particular and East Providence in general, 1893 was a critical turning point. In that year the Richmond Paper Company was put up for sale. Phillips quickly saw the business advantage the location on the east side of the Seekonk River afforded. The Providence and Worcester railroad ran right by the paper mill. The site was even equipped with a small, wooden freight station. Thus Phillips could receive his copper wire by rail at the door of his mill, insulate it, and easily ship it to his customers. Furthermore, the Seekonk River offered easy water transportation.

The Phillipsdale train depot

Buoyed by new demands for his product, which stemmed from the need for overhead wires to operate electric streetcars, Phillips bought the brick and wooden buildings and homes which had made up the paper mill complex, and the American Electrical Works moved to East Providence. At the same time, the village was rechristened Phillipsdale. A year later, in 1894, a direct trolley line to Providence was opened to provide service for the residents and workers of the bustling village. Company clambakes were now shifted to the Pomham Club in Riverside.

In 1895 nearly 700 workers were employed at the American Electrical Works. Many of them lived in a huge boarding house, the "Sullivan House," which was located at the bend where Roger Williams Avenue heads toward Pawtucket Avenue. In 1898 Phillips purchased the Old Stone House at Clyde Mills from the Rumford Chemical Works and converted it into a boarding house for his workers.

Company housing was also built along Roger Williams and Bourne Avenues. The *Providence Journal* reported in 1900: "The American

Electrical Works has erected more houses this past year than has been erected elsewhere in the whole town, and they are good structures, partly two tenements, yet many single tenement houses. It is understood that a large number are to be erected there this coming season."

The streets which ran through the new residential area were named after Phillips' granddaughters, Ruth and Miriam. Nearby, at the corner of Roger Williams and Bourne Avenues, was the company store. The dwelling on Bourne Avenue next to the store housed the superintendent of the American Electrical Works and the company doctor. Several

The Phillipsdale police station

hundred yards south on Roger Williams stood Phillipsdale's only school. This small wooden structure (presently being used by Grace Episcopal Church as a parish center) contained only the first four grades. Phillipsdale youth who wanted more education had to attend the Union Primary School nearly three miles away in Rumford.

As Phillips was expanding his mill village, another major company moved into the area. In 1899 Frank Sayles, who had important textile interests in the Blackstone Valley, opened the Glenlyon Bleachery adjacent to the American Electrical Works. Sayles also built a number of brick tenements along Roger Williams Avenue.

The Washburn Wire Company

As the Glenlyon Bleachery began operating, Phillips was laying the groundwork for a new mill – the Washburn Wire Company – in Phillipsdale. Almost from the founding of his American Electrical Works, Phillips bought the copper wire he insulated from the Washburn and Moen Company of Worcester, Massachusetts. In the 1890's the Washburn Company became part of a national corporation called the American Steel and Wire Company. But Charles Washburn, a descendant of the original founders of Washburn and Moen, was dissatisfied with the new arrangement and left the corporation.

Washburn convinced Eugene Phillips, his close friend and business associate, to join him as a partner in a new company, the Washburn Wire Company. Phillips agreed, and in 1900 the American Electrical Works was absorbed by Washburn Wire. To accommodate the new company, more land was purchased adjacent to the buildings at Phillipsdale.

From the Agawam Finishing Company, Phillips and Washburn acquired the land surrounding Omega Pond, including exclusive title to water rights. While Phillips continued to run the American Electrical Works as a division of the new Washburn Wire Company, workers began to construct a steel plant across the railroad tracks in 1900, under the watchful eye of Washburn.

The Agawam Country Club as seen from the Penn Central railroad tracks, with the tennis courts in the foreground: Agawam is the Indian for "low land lying close to a river."

The steel mill began production in August of 1901. Two open hearth furnaces burned constantly and, as one writer has put it, "Phillipsdale became a miniature Pittsburgh." Phillips served as general manager of the Washburn Wire Company and both of its divisions – the American Electrical Works and the steel mill – prospered. By 1904, for instance, the American Electrical Works had established sales offices in Boston, New York and Chicago. In that same year, Washburn resigned from the company and left Phillips as the major stockholder.

During these years of success for his company, Phillips made one final contribution to the community. He decided to construct a church to serve the villagers and to honor the memory of his daughter, Grace, who had died at an early age. Grace Memorial Church on Roger Williams

Avenue was built and dedicated in 1903. Phillips died two years later and left his stock in the company to his two sons, Eugene, Jr., and Frank.

In the decade or so before World War I, the young men found themselves as busy as their father had been. The introduction of electrical streetlighting around 1909 proved to be a major boon to the business. The company was deluged with orders from electric companies, and had to supply increasingly large demands, as well, for underground cable, telephone and telegraph wire. As a result, new wire and steel mills were added to the Phillipsdale plant. Also at this time the Washburn Company, along with other manufacturers of copper products, was fined by the federal government for price fixing and practices in restraint of trade.

The Agawam Hunt Club

In addition to the American Electrical Works, Washburn Wire and the Glenlyon Bleachery, several small manufacturers such as the Phillipsdale Paper Mill and the L.A. Lockwood Cotton Mill crowded around Omega Pond. Thus in 1909 the *Providence Journal* summarized developments in this "ragged edge of Rumford" during the previous fifteen years: "There is probably no other village in the State, and there are few in New England, which have had such rapid growth in an industrial way as the little settlement on the easterly bank of the Seekonk River." From a barely discernible village with a few hundred scattered people in the early 1890's, Phillipsdale had become by 1909 "the largest manufacturing center in East Providence, a thriving community in which about 2,000 persons live in model factory tenements or homes of their own."

More important, Phillipsdale was the location of the Washburn Wire Company, "which with the single exception of the N.Y.N.H. and Hartford Railroad is the largest taxpayer in the town." World War I would bring further prosperity to Phillipsdale and Washburn Wire. As countries began to arm themselves, the need for the company's products increased. War orders kept hundreds of workers in Phillipsdale on overtime. To meet the demand a new open hearth furnace which produced over 2,000 pounds of steel a month was erected at Washburn Wire.

In less than fifty years the company had grown from a one man operation to a major producer of copper products and steel. Washburn Wire had become the largest employer and the largest manufacturing operation in East Providence. The land on which Roger Williams had first attempted to establish his exile settlement was now the home of the millhands who populated the compact village of Phillipsdale.

An overview of Phillipsdale today, as seen from the train trestle on Roger Williams Avenue

In focusing on the commercial and industrial transformation of Watchemoket, Rumford and Phillipsdale between 1865 and World War I, the reader may be left with the impression that agriculture, once the backbone of the economy, was no longer vital to East Providence. This would be far from the truth. George Wilson's attempt to combine manufacturing and agriculture in Rumford suggests that farming was still an important part of the town's economy.

Indeed, late in the nineteenth century one writer reported that East Providence had more than 100 farms with a cash value in land and buildings of over a million dollars. Vegetables were cultivated and the town's potato crop alone averaged about 20,000 bushels a year. Carrots, beets, cabbage, turnips and strawberries were other important farm products raised on a large scale. Moreover, a number of dairy farms provided milk, butter and cheese for the inhabitants of the town and nearby Providence.

The largest farm in East Providence belonged to the Kent family, and in 1901 it covered well over 400 acres along Pawtucket Avenue in the present day Kent Heights section of the city. The Kent family grew

An old postcard view of the Kent Heights Store on Pawtucket Avenue, with the horse-drawn store wagon in the foreground

The A. J. Kent homestead, with the East Providence waterworks tower, was the center of a 400 acre farm in 1901.

strawberries, hay and other products, and was also involved in dairy farming. But the Kent farm was known throughout the state for the large quantity of excellent potatoes it produced.

Although steadily declining in number as the town industrialized, such commercial farming operations remained part of East Providence's economy well into the twentieth century. Not far from the Kent farm stood one thinly populated agricultural area largely undisturbed by heavy industry even as late as World War I. But this fourth village of East Providence also went through a period which produced dramatic changes, although these changes differed from those that affected the other areas of the town. The people who made their money in places like Watchemoket, Rumford and Phillipsdale, spent it in places like Riverside.

VI

Riverside: "The Coney Island of New England," 1865-1917

From the time of the Wannamoisett purchase in 1645 down to the Civil War, the shore land from Watchemoket to Bullocks Point had remained a sparsely settled farming and fishing area. When East Providence was incorporated in 1862, no more than a few hundred of its residents made the coastal village, which was soon to be renamed Riverside, their home. Most of these residents earned a livelihood by fishing or farming, many engaging in both.

The white settlers had first learned of the plentiful supply of shellfish in the area from the Wampanoag Indians who established their summer encampment on the shore at Wannamoisett. More than two centuries later, the waters of Narragansett Bay, which washed the shores of Wannamoisett, still contained an abundant supply of edible sea treasures. Succulent clams, quahogs and oysters were harvested by Wannamoisett residents and sold in the center of town or in Providence. Arnold Medberry, for instance, a farmer in Wannamoisett, brought his plow to the shore line, turned over the sand as if he were going to plant a crop, and began picking up clams by the handsful. He loaded the shellfish on an oxcart and headed for Providence where he had little difficulty selling his entire catch. Since many of the permanent inhabitants of Wannamoisett were involved in shellfishing, the "townies," that is, the residents of the central districts of East Providence, referred to Medberry and his neighbors as "clamdiggers," a derogatory term comparable to the pejorative hayseed. Many of these "clamdiggers" would soon realize sizable profits by selling some of their farm land to real estate developers.

Already by the early nineteenth century, individuals had begun to build summer homes in Wannamoisett, causing the population of the area to double to about five or six hundred in July and August. To be sure, most of the early summer retreats were little more than shacks. The summer colonists who lived in these structures were supplemented by weekend campers who pitched tents along the shore. The Providence and Warren railroad ran through the area beginning in the 1850's, stopping at Lewis Station and making Wannamoisett more accessible than it had been in the past. Developers moved into the village soon after the arrival of the railroad. Summer recreation facilities first appeared in the southern-most region of Wannamoisett, at the head of Bullocks Point, in the 1860's, and for the next several decades followed the coastline northward toward Watchemoket, earning this three or four mile waterfront strip recognition as the "Coney Island of New England."

The transformation of the peaceful farming and fishing village into a fashionable recreation and resort area began with little fanfare around 1860, with the construction of the Vue de l'Eau Hotel. It was in this large structure, fronting on Narragansett Bay, that the newly incorporated Town of East Providence held its celebration ball in 1862. At the time the area surrounding the Vue de l'Eau was called Cedar Grove because of the numerous stately cedar trees which graced the landscape.

The Captain Willett Arms Apartments at Chimney Corners today marks the site of the Willett home.

Other parts of Wannamoisett were: Lewis Station, Chimney Corners, Peck's Corner, Pleasant Bluffs, Sabin's Point, Sherman's Station and Pomham.

In the 1860's the area had only two roads – Bullocks Point Avenue running north and south and Lincoln Avenue running east and west. Both of these streets were covered with oyster shells which, if not an easy surface to walk or ride on, at least supplied good drainage during rainstorms, preventing the roads from turning into mud as they did in other sections of East Providence.

In the late 1860's and 1870's new resort facilities similar to the Vue de l'Eau, as well as campsites, cottages and clambake houses, began to appear in the Cedar Grove vicinity – at least as rapidly, it must have seemed to the resident clamdiggers of the area, as the changing of the tides. The Pomham House, which was equipped with its own wharf to receive boarders coming across the Bay by steamship, opened in 1867. A short while later, developer Hiram Maxfield, who was better known as the "shore king," built perhaps the most successful resort complex on the eastern side of Narragansett Bay. "Silver Spring," which opened in 1869, consisted of a hotel, a shore dinner hall and summer cottages. These buildings were painted white and could be clearly seen from the Bay. Steamships, constantly docked at the resort's wharf, unloaded passengers and an equally heavy traffic arrived in sweltering railroad cars and, later, in electric streetcars.

Somewhat less successful than Silver Spring, but equally interesting, were the What Cheer House and the Riverside Hotel. The former contained forty rooms, all of which were well ventilated by cool ocean breezes. Wide porches on all sides of the building overlooked rolling lawns that stretched to the shore. But although the building was beautiful and the location was ideal (it was only five miles, about a fifteen minute train ride, from Providence to Lewis Station and then a five minute walk to the vacation spot), the What Cheer House apparently ran into financial problems during its first years. It changed hands several times and finally began to prosper under a new name, the Bullocks Point Hotel. But this success was shortlived. Soon the once placid atmosphere of Cedar Grove was ruffled by the cacophony of the midway at nearby Crescent Park, forcing the owner of the hotel to sell out to the operators of the amusement park who renamed the building the Crescent Park House.

This postcard scene of the Crescent Park Landing carries the message of a turn-of-the-century visitor.

The Summer Hotel in Riverside was crowded with 19th century guests.

The Riverside Hotel, built a few years after the What Cheer House, rivaled "Silver Spring" in size and grandeur. Four stories high, with a wharf that measured 1,300 feet in length and 40 feet in width, and possessing a huge ballroom overlooking Narragansett Bay, the Riverside Hotel was one of the most ambitious resort projects of its day. Perhaps it was too ambitious, for after a short while the hotel was dismantled, loaded on barges and floated to Nantucket where it served tourists for years to come.

Stiff competition was doubtless one of the factors in the failure of the Riverside Hotel. By around 1880, a nighttime traveler on Narragansett Bay could see the darkened eastern shore studded with the lights and flickering fires from numerous boarding houses, cottages and campsites. In addition to the Pomham House, Silver Spring, the Bullocks Point Hotel and the Riverside Hotel, vacationers could choose from among the East Providence Hotel, Paton's Hotel, Pleasant Bluff, Cedar Grove, Crescent Bluff, Smith Palace, Ocean Cottage and Camp White. Nearly all of these vacation establishments rented their patrons rooms, cottages and campsites and provided opportunities for swimming, fish-

The Shore Dinner Hall: one of the many old establishments that welcomed guests to a typical New England dinner.

ing, dancing and sailing. Some visitors came to the area simply to have a shore dinner in one of Wannamoisett's many shore dinner halls, or to participate in a famous Rhode Island clambake.

In the midst of all these commercial vacation spots stood one of America's oldest private clubs specializing in the art of the clambake. The Squantum Club was built in 1871 and received a charter a year later, but its history was nearly forty years old by then. Since 1835 two groups of prominent Providence men had been perfecting the clambake, a legacy of the Wampanoag Indians, in annual outings.

The cannon and ship's wheel at the Squantum Club

One group was comprised primarily of merchants in the South Water Street area who journeyed to a location near Pawtuxet for their clambakes. In 1868 they joined a second group of merchants who had been classmates at Benefit Street High School, and who had for a number of years been making annual clambake outings to Huckleberry Island in Narragansett Bay, right off the coast from East Providence's growing resort district.

Shortly after the merger of the two groups, the owners of Huckleberry Island put a stop to the use of their land for clambakes. The forty-four members of the Squantum Association then decided to purchase about three acres of land just to the north of the island where they could build their own club. To finance the project they established a fifty dollar membership fee and sold a small number of shares for one hundred dollars each. The first clubhouse was completed in 1871, and another was built two years later.

The Squantum Club continued to expand in the following years, purchasing more land and erecting new buildings. It became the most famous eating place in East Providence. Whenever a dignitary visited the town (Presidents Arthur and Taft, for example) they were entertained at the Squantum Club, and dined on its gourmet cuisine.

The prestige of the Squantum Club and the popularity of East Providence's vacation district in the decade or so after the Civil War were

The terraced dining hall of the Squantum Club, overlooking the river

graphically portrayed by one contemporary observer. Writing in *Picturesque Rhode Island,* Wilfred Munroe described the scene at Wannamoisett on a typical summer day:

> The numerous trains of the Bristol railway are often stopping at its stations; excursion steamers decked with flags and streamers gay, are ever landing great loads of human freight upon its bending piers. Silver Spring is the destination of most of these excursionists. Some of them stop at Ocean Cottage. A few favored mortals enter the great well-kept grounds over which the flag of the Squantum Club waves enticingly. The(ir) steps are all turned towards one common goal. A 'genuine Rhode Island Clambake.'

During the height of the vacation season, well over ten thousand people sought refuge from the oppressive city heat along the breezy shores of Wannamoisett.

Some were boarders, others were campers. A select group owned summer cottages while still others simply sought a refreshing afternoon outing on the glittering white sand of one of the area's several beaches. "On Pawtucket Aveune on Sundays during the shore season," the East Providence Police Department reported in 1885, "there is great demand for several officers, some mounted, to keep in order the tumultuous excursionists who throng the highway and misbehave themselves to the great annoyance of the residents along the way." The department went on to inform the town council that the single police officer in charge of the resort round was "almost daily compelled to risk his life in the discharge of (his) duty, for many of the visitors are hard characters." As a result of these complaints, the town council appointed East Providence's first auxiliary police whose job it was to help keep order on weekends in Wannamoisett.

At the same time that outsiders were making greater and greater use of the area's summer recreation facilities and causing new problems for town officials, the permanent population of Cedar Grove, Peck's Corners, Pleasant Bluffs and other sections of Wannamoisett began to grow slowly but steadily. The first attempt of real estate developers to transform the village's farmland into residential plots was made in 1871.

General Lysander Flagg, the builder of the ill-fated Riverside Hotel, formed a partnership with several businessmen from his hometown of Pawtucket. These investors purchased three farms and began laying out

The stone marker and Whitcomb Farm house

house lots. The strange design of this small community, which modern residents of East Providence have come to know as "The Maze," was the brainchild of General Flagg. Streets were laid out in semicircles designed to replicate the contour of the nearby coastline. The inspiration for the residential labyrinth had come to Flagg while he was traveling out West. He had seen a community planned in the intricate fashion that would come to characterize "The Maze."

The winding streets of Flagg's plot were named after the presidents of the United States up to that time. Other streets, which were added later as the development spread out beyond the original maze, bore the names of secretaries of state and governors of Rhode Island. Throughout the plot Flagg and his partners built a number of houses which were put up for sale.

By 1875, then, the village which only a decade or so before had only two streets, both covered with oyster shells, now had a number of roads lined with houses and trees. The year-round population of the area had doubled to between five and six hundred. To these people and others with more than just a monetary interest in the community, rapid real estate development had begun to put things out of control.

An old scene of ice-cutters at work on Bowen's Pond, now called Willett Pond

The growth of the village was outrunning the town's ability to supply vital public services. (Witness the complaints of the the East Providence Police Department, for example.) Then, too, there was the possibility that the resort district would go the way of other summer recreation areas. Perhaps shacks of all shapes and sizes would come to dot the shore while more aesthetically constructed summer cottages would begin to be converted to all-year homes, creating a sprawling, crazy quilt of beachfront architecture which one can still see in old resort areas. One thinks here of sections of the Bullocks Point area in Riverside, or nearby West Barrington, or Oakland Beach on the opposite side of the

Bay.

To put reins on the seemingly unbridled growth of Wannamoisett in general and of Cedar Grove in particular, ordinary citizens and prominent businessmen of the village formed the Riverside Improvement Society in 1878. One of the first tasks of the new group was to change officially the name of the Cedar Grove community to Riverside, a name which gradually came to apply to the entire resort area. The Society then functioned as a citizens' council attempting to promote not simply the lucrative summer recreation industry but the welfare of the community as a whole.

There was clearly a need for such an organization in 1878, for the growth of the permanent population of Riverside required new provisions for education, religion and municipal services. Most of the early civic improvements in Riverside occurred in the area where Flagg had built his residential community and were spearheaded by people connected with this real estate development. Flagg and one of his partners, James Davis, for example, built and provided the early financial support for the first church in Riverside. Union Chapel, a non-denominational house of worship, was opened in the summer of 1872. Up to that time the permanent residents of the village as well as the summer visitors who wished to attend Sunday services were obliged to travel to Barrington and worship at the Congregational Church in that town – a journey which year-round Congregational residents found uninviting, let alone vacationing Episcopalians, Baptists and Methodists!

Thus each summer from July to September Flagg and Davis hired a minister and opened Union Chapel to all Protestants who wished to attend. (Catholics had to travel to Watchemoket's Church of the Sacred Heart if they wished to attend Mass. Later a mission was established to serve them. Saint Brendan's, the third Catholic parish in East Providence, was not organized in Riverside until 1909.) To accommodate the growing numbers of full-time residents of Riverside, Union Chapel began in 1874 to hold Sunday services year round. Both Flagg and Davis hoped that their chapel would fill a religious void in the community until separate denominational churches could be established.

By 1881, the mission of Union Chapel had been fulfilled. Two churches, one Congregational and the other Episcopalian, had been organized. The founders of Union Chapel, therefore, sold their building to the members of the newly formed Riverside Congregational Church.

The second house of worship to open in Riverside in 1881 was St.

Mark's Episcopal Church. For several years prior to this the Episcopalian residents of the area who did not wish to attend Union Chapel met in the home of their fellow religionists where services were conducted by the Reverend William M. Chapin, Rector of St. John's Episcopal Church in Barrington. As the worshipers grew in number, it became increasingly difficult for services to be held in a private dwelling. Hence, in 1881, the Episcopalians leased an old schoolhouse, which they later purchased, and called it St. Marks' Mission Chapel. Four years later a new church and rectory were opened and the Reverend Frederick Thompson became St. Mark's first rector.

What General Lysander Flagg was to the early religious history of Riverside, his brother and siter-in-law, Mr. and Mrs. John Flagg, were to its early educational history. Both were schoolteachers in their native Shrewsbury, Massachusetts, when General Flagg invited them to take up residence in Riverside after he had constructed "The Maze." At that

The Riverside Girl Scout House once served as the area's first school

time the village had only a one-room school (now the Riverside Girl Scout House) and that was a half mile away on Willett Avenue. For awhile, Mr. and Mrs. Flagg jointly taught the Riverside pupils of all ages who attended this school.

When the school age population expanded in the 1870's, the town leased a commercial building on Turner Avenue and turned it into a classroom. (This was the same building which the parishioners of St. Mark's used as a church prior to 1885.) Finally, these makeshift quarters were abandoned in 1880 when the Turner Avenue School was built. By this time, Mr. and Mrs. Flagg were no longer teaching in the village's original school on Willett Avenue. However, Mrs. Flagg had formed a school of her own. Since she had been a high school principal in Massachusetts, and since East Providence had no high school at the time (not until 1885, one will recall), Mrs. Flagg started a private school in her home and taught students high school subjects. She conducted this school for twenty-five years (1874-1899).

In addition to these advances in education, a library, the third in East Providence, was opened in Riverside in 1881. This library began much as the town's other two had. Largely through the efforts of the Reverend William Chapin of St. Mark's Church, a few hundred volumes were collected in 1882. Two years later, the Riverside Free Public Lib-

The Riverside Library opened in 1881.

rary Association was incorporated and by 1889 it possessed more than fifteen hundred volumes. Finally, in 1894 a building was constructed on Lincoln Avenue, and the library moved into its new home.

A short distance from the library, and in the heart of the growing residential district stood the recently opened station of Riverside's volunteer fire department. The Narragansett Engine Company was formed in 1878 and stored its equipment in a barn on Turner Avenue. This structure also housed a district police station.

The Narragansett Engine Company: formed in 1878, it first stored its equipment in a barn on Turner Avenue.

The combination fire and police station looked out on a small business square bordering on "The Maze." At first only a single grocery store, which doubled as a post office, served the residents of the area. But in the 1880's and early 1890's substantial business buildings were erected. The Grube Block was constructed in 1886 and was followed by Paton's Block, opened six years later. Sometime in between, Levi Winchester, who had operated the village's old grocery store, built the Winchester Block which, among other things, contained a hall that was used for political meetings and as Riverside's polling place.

By around 1890, then, the year-round residents of Riverside could no longer be condescendingly dismissed as "clamdiggers" by their fellow townspeople. The village had made considerable progress in establishing educational, religious and cultural institutions and much needed public services were now available. Furthermore, a small business district provided Riverside with drug, grocery and dry goods stores. Yet most people still came to Riverside not to live but to indulge. The area continued to be known primarily as a resort district. Indeed, while the institutional seeds (schools, churches, a library, police and fire stations and stores) of a permanent community were being planted, the summer recreation industry was in full bloom.

Not only did Riverside's numerous hotels, cottages, campsites, shore dinner halls and beaches continue to prosper in the late nineteenth and early twentieth centuries, but a new dimension was added to these vacation offerings. The opening of amusement parks secured the area's reputation as the "Coney Island of New England." Crescent Park, Boyden Heights and, for a very brief period, Vanity Fair made Riverside truly a summer playground.

The Vanity Fair bandstand, in a postcard scene dated 1907, is today the site of the Silver Spring Golf Course.

In 1886, George Boyden, the former owner of Riverside's Vue de l'Eau Hotel, opened an amusement park adjacent to the Bullock's Point Hotel (formerly the What Cheer House). The amusement park undermined the business of the boarding house. Day and night a constant din from Boyden's establishment hovered over the shaded grounds

The Grand Ballroom at Vanity Fair

of the Bullock's Point Hotel, disturbing afternoon nappers, early night sleepers, and those who simply sought the quiet of the establishment's large screened-in porches on a hot summer evening. Once in the peaceful dark of night, boarders could look out from these porches and, following a flickering firefly against a pitch-black background, be tranquilized by the rhythmic hum of crickets. But now the night sky was flooded with the glare of lights from the amusement park while the screams and laughter of its patrons drowned out more soothing sounds.

For several years James Woodward, proprietor of the Bullock's Point Hotel, watched his business decline and feuded with Boyden whom he blamed for his difficulties. Finally, Woodward threw up his hands and sold out to his enemy. The hotel was renamed the Crescent Park House and amusement rides and activities expanded almost to its doorstep. The building was eventually torn down to provide a parking lot for visitors to the amusement park.

After having dispossessed Woodward, Boyden sold Crescent Park to the Hope Land Company which, in turn, signed the property over to Colonel R.A. Harrington, proprietor of the rival Rocky Point Amusement Park on the opposite side of Narragansett Bay. While these transactions were taking place, the man who would soon lease the property and develop it into a first rate amusement facility had come to work at Crescent Park.

Charles I. D. Looff was a woodcarver in a New York City furniture factory. He spent his spare time in the basement of his house where he carved wooden horses for a hobby. After long years of hard work he produced the first steam powered carousel and sold it to the amusement park at Coney Island. Looff built a second carousel which he sold to Crescent Park. Then, in 1894, he moved to Riverside to operate his carousel and to construct others in a barn on the grounds of the amusement park.

An early postcard scene of the amusement area at Crescent Park

Shortly after, Looff acquired a lease to Crescent Park and began promoting it as the "Coney Island of New England," a designation which came to apply to the entire Riverside summer recreation area. By the early 1900's Crescent Park was recognized by residents of New England as the leading amusement park in the region. The testimony of one group of Bostonians who were planning an outing in 1913 illustrates the lofty reputation of Crescent Park.

The Filene Cooperative Association (the exact nature of the group is unclear, but it was apparently an organization of workers in Filene Department Stores) reported in 1913 that its field day committee had surveyed all the amusement parks in New England before deciding where to hold its annual outing. Then the members of the committee unanimously chose Crescent Park and sang its praises to their fellow workers: "Crescent Park is the largest and most beautiful Seashore Pleasure Park on the Atlantic Coast. It has six hundred acres of woodland, field and seashore." The amusement park had a dance hall (later called the Alhambra Ballroom, easily one of the largest in New England), a gigantic midway, bathing and shore dinner facilities and band concerts. "In fact," the field day committee excitedly informed the other members of the Filene Cooperative Association, "Crescent Park holds more opportunities for a good time for you and all your family and friends than any other place on the map." Clearly, Looff had in a very short period turned Crescent Park into a major success, relegating Warwick's Rocky Point Amusement Park to a position of secondary importance.

All of this was accomplished by Looff and, after his death, by members of his family who continued to operate Crescent Park, while competitors attempted to chisel out corners of the amusement park market in Riverside. George Boyden, for example, shortly after selling Crescent Park, started a new amusement enterprise called Boyden Heights. He remodelled a shore resort, Ocean Cottage, which was located on a bluff overlooking Narragansett Bay to the north of Crescent Park. Boyden Heights contained rides, a shore dinner hall, and a very popular dance hall. Still Boyden's establishment was no match for Crescent Park.

For a brief period, though, another amusement venture, perhaps the most grandiose of its time, threatened the supremacy of Crescent Park.

A postcard scene of "Shooting the Chutes"

Vanity Fair opened in 1907 amidst considerable excitement and rosy predictions for the future of Riverside's summer recreation industry. Within a few years a promoter's dream had turned into a financial nightmare. And, as in a nightmare, the residents of East Providence woke up one morning and found that Vanity Fair had vanished, the work of a young, unwitting arsonist who saved the community supporters of the amusement park from further embarassment.

On May 25, 1907 more than twenty-five thousand people came by steamship, trolley and train to a spot just north of Silver Spring to participate in opening day festivities at Vanity Fair. The common folk were joined by the mayors of Providence, Pawtucket, Woonsocket and Fall River who described the occasion as an historic event for the southeastern New England region. At the time their enthusiastic support of Vanity Fair appeared to be well placed.

The promotion plans called for a 40 acre amusement park which would contain diverse types of entertainment from rides to circus acts and wild west shows. When completed, Vanity Fair was intended to be the largest amusement park in the world, an early twentieth century version of Disneyland. But largely because of the objections of many East Providence residents, the original plans were far from completed when Vanity Fair opened in 1907.

Nevertheless, the unfinished amusement park was still an impressive complex of rides and buildings which gave visitors a clear picture of the ambitious plans of the developers. Much of the park, for example, was built on a massive boardwalk which had required two million feet of lumber to construct. On the boardwalk there was the conventional amusement park fare – rides, a dance hall, and a shore dinner hall. But there was also much more.

A number of attractions were in the planning stage while others were in operation by 1907: a scenic railroad, a wild west show, an Indian congress, a Japanese village, a children's theater, a circus and a wild animal area. But the most popular event at Vanity Fair was an act called "Fighting the Flames." A five story building was erected where a simulated fire occurred each day. As smoke billowed from the structure, actresses leaned out its windows and cried for help. Soon their rescuers appeared with a horse-drawn fire engine. Ladders were lifted to the building and its occupants were carried to safety. Others jumped into a waiting net or into the arms of a fireman as the crowd cheered in delight. So realistic was the action involved in "Fighting the Flames"

The East Providence Dock stands on the site of the old Vanity Fair.

that participants were seriously injured from time to time.

In spite of the popularity of "Fighting the Flames," and the elaborate and diverse nature of the entertainment at Vanity Fair, the amusement park was in financial straits almost from the outset. By 1908, construction had stopped and the developers were out of money. A year later a new Vanity Fair Company was formed only to file for bankruptcy in 1910. The residents of East Providence who had opposed the construction of the now-abandoned amusement park composed a little jingle which became as popular as "Fighting the Flames" had once been:

> Vanity Fair, Vanity Fair,
> Everything open,
> And nobody there.

Finally, in 1912, while rummaging through one of Vanity Fair's buildings and perhaps reliving a warm summer afternoon or night at the amusement park, a young boy started a fire which caused substantial damage.

It was now evident to all that this real life "Fighting the Flames" had sealed Vanity Fair's fate. It never opened again. In 1915 the Standard Oil Corporation of New York (Socony) purchased the Vanity Fair site and by 1917 eight kerosene storage tanks had taken over the amuse-

An old view of the Standard Oil Office Building in Riverside: the company purchased the Vanity Fair site in 1915.

The Standard Oil Co. bridge on Pawtucket Avenue

ment park's midway.

The opening of Vanity Fair represents the highwater mark of Riverside's development as a summer resort area. Even though the venture was a failure, for promoters to think on such a large scale suggests that Riverside was at the height of its reputation as a vacation spot. However, a gradual decline began around the time that the Standard Oil Company moved into the area. Soon this slow descent would be accelerated by the Depression, and by the hurricane of 1938.

VII
War, Depression and Recovery, 1917-1945

The outbreak of World War I in the middle of 1914 took Americans by surprise. Because the United States was isolated from Europe by several thousand miles of ocean, few Americans had been aware of Old World economic and political rivalries which had been seething for decades. Within less than three years, however, the United States was drawn into the conflict.

Well before President Woodrow Wilson's declaration of war in early April, 1917, an army was in the process of being recruited. Quotas were established for communities which would be filled by a draft if enough volunteers were not found. In East Providence the first quota call was filled entirely by volunteer enlistments, with subsequent calls being filled by a combination of volunteers and draftees. Altogether, 804 of East Providence's young men would serve their country in war.

When America entered the war, Germany and her allies clearly had the upper hand. With more soldiers in uniform, and with a successful campaign of submarine warfare backing up the land war, Germany, Austria-Hungary and Italy appeared to be moving toward victory. Thus America's declaration of war came at a crucial time. It raised the morale of Great Britain and her allies and, more important, the American army brought to their side fresh recruits who erased the numerical advantage that the opposing forces held. A year and a half after American entry into the war, the fighting stopped. On November 11, 1918, Germany signed an armistice.

American losses totaled 48,000 killed in battle, nearly 3,000 missing in action and 56,000 dead from disease. Twenty-three of these casualties were young men from East Providence. On the front of the town hall officials placed a plaque in memory of East Providence's dead servicemen.

Those who returned alive were greeted like heroes. A huge victory arch was erected in Exchange Place in Providence, and Rhode Island war veterans arrived at the railroad station and paraded through the arch while bands played and the crowd cheered. East Providence veterans then returned to their hometown to participate in a local celebration.

The streets of Watchemoket were decorated, and the returning servicemen formed the most important part of a large parade which followed a route through the center of town. Next the veterans journeyed to the Pomham Club where they were treated to an old-fashioned Rhode Island seafood dinner at the town's expense. They were entertained with war songs ("Over There" and "Pack up your Troubles"), and presented with certificates of appreciation for their service in the war. It was now mid-afternoon, but the festivities were not yet over. The servicemen headed for Grovesnor Field to watch a baseball game that had been scheduled for their benefit. Finally, the official celebration ended with a ball at Hunts' Mills in honor of the servicemen.

The ten years from the return of the soldiers in 1919 to the stock market crash which signalled the Great Depression in 1929 marked a period of continued growth for East Providence. From a population of 18,584 in 1915, the town increased to nearly 22,000 residents by 1920. This figure climbed to over 26,000 in 1925 and almost 30,000 by 1929. Major changes accompanied this expansion of the population. While Rumford and Phillipsdale followed the lines of their early development as mill villages, Riverside and Watchemoket were diverted from their historical courses.

The winds of change blew most forcefully in Riverside. In the first place, Socony continued to transform the northern region of the village's shoreline. After constructing storage tanks on the site of Vanity Fair in 1917, the company launched a study on the feasibility of erecting a refinery nearby. On the recommendation of this study, the company purchased nearly 1,200 more acres of land in Riverside.

Construction of the refinery was launched in 1919 when 800 men began draining, clearing and filling what was largely swampland between Pawtucket Avenue and Ruhlins River. Socony laid a mile and a half of tracks from the New Haven Railroad line at Vanity Fair to the location of the refinery. Not only soil and rock to fill the swampland but men and equipment were transported by flat cars from Pawtucket Avenue to the construction site. Eight pipelines were built connecting the refinery to the storage tanks on the shore.

By 1920 the refinery was in full operation. Tankers carried crude oil from Mexico to Socony's docks in Riverside. Their cargo was then pumped into the storage tanks, and transferred by pipeline to the refinery where the crude oil was converted into gasoline and distributed all over New England.

The long-range plans of the company called for East Providence to be one of the largest, perhaps the largest, refinery on the Atlantic Coast. But when Socony acquired another oil company which had a refinery in Texas, close to oil fields and in a cheap labor market, the plans to make East Providence a major refining location were dropped. Nonetheless, Socony's plant in East Providence continued to grow. A major pipeline was laid all the way to Springfield, Massachusetts and Hartford, Connecticut and supplied petroleum products to those areas. The East Providence refinery then began producing asphalt and became one of the main suppliers of that product in New England. More important, Socony brought jobs and tax revenues to the town. For years the refinery would be one of the largest employers and taxpayers in East Providence.

In addition to the growth of Socony, Riverside experienced other changes in the 1920's and '30's. By then many of the original resort hotels and boarding houses were fifty or sixty years old, and falling into disrepair. Some were left to decay until the Hurricane of 1938 washed away their remains. Others fell into the hands of unscrupulous operators and were turned into dens of prostitution or "speakeasies" where liquor was sold in defiance of Prohibition laws. In short, Riverside's glittering shoreline began to tarnish, and after a decade of depression and a battering hurricane, much of it would turn to rust.

Only the Narragansett Terrace area at the extreme southern end of Riverside remained largely immune to these developments. A small upper middle class summer colony, comprised primarily of businessmen, lawyers and doctors, had begun to form at Narragansett Terrace around the turn of the century.

Just before World War I the residents of the area established a community improvement association which in subsequent years played a crucial role in protecting the isolated watering place from the deleterious forces that were affecting other sections of Riverside. Throughout the 1920's and 1930's, Narragansett Terrace remained a prestigious community. Perhaps its most famous resident at that time was Norman Case, who served as lieutenant governor and then governor of Rhode Island between 1927 and 1932.

In at least one respect the history of Narragansett Terrace and of Riverside as a whole ran parallel during the 1920's. Both the small, affluent hamlet and the larger resort village of which it was a part experienced an upsurge of permanent residents. A transportation revolution was mostly responsible for this development.

Like much of America in the 1920's, Riverside – indeed, all of East Providence – felt the effects of the almost incredible increase in the number and use of the automobile. No longer simply a luxury of the rich, by the 1920's moderate income families could afford a car. In 1900, for example, only 4,000 cars were produced. By 1929 this figure had risen to nearly five million. Henry Ford's mass production of relatively inexpensive models was the principal cause of this stunning increase.

In turn the automobile was responsible for other major social changes. The transformation of Riverside from a vacation district to a residential suburban area of Providence, for example, was facilitated in the 1920's by the automobile. It was now much easier for a person to work in Providence and live in Riverside. Thus the prosperity of the post-World War I years could be seen in East Providence not only in the increasing number of automobiles but also in a housing boom in areas like Riverside.

Watchemoket felt another ramification of the sudden popularity of the automobile. A new mode of transportation and increasing traffic required modernized roads, highways and bridges. By the mid-1920's the State of Rhode Island had concluded that the much-traveled Washington Bridge needed to be rebuilt. Since the automobile had replaced many of the horsedrawn wagons which crossed the bridge daily, a sturdier structure was required.

The State decided to erect a large concrete bridge which would connect on the East Providence side with Routes 6, 44 and the Barrington (now Veteran's Memorial) Parkway. Like most progress, this advance in transportation proved to be a mixed blessing. The bridge required a wide expanse of land on the East Providence side where the Watchemoket business district was located. Hence, the new Washington Bridge brought about the demise of the town's bustling waterfront business community. Eviction notices went out to establishments in the area around 1927 and they began scattering in all directions. In a short while, the heart of Watchemoket was severed by what must have seemed to many a concrete monster.

At almost the same time a less ambiguous advance was made in the town's water supply. For years the residents in the general area of the town hall on Taunton Avenue were part of the Watchemoket Fire District which supplied homes and businesses with water from the City of Pawtucket. Most of the remaining areas of the town belonged to the East Providence Fire District and received water from the East Providence Water Company, a privately owned operation adjacent to Hunts' Mills which pumped water from the Ten Mile River.

The pumping station at Hunts' Mills, shown here in an old postcard scene, served the community until 1969.

In 1928 the Frank Sayles Finishing Plant, the owner of the East Providence Water Company, sold forty acres of land next to Hunts' Mills along with water rights to the Ten Mile River. The town then established a public water department. A dam, reservoir and pumping station were built at the scenic site of Hunts' Mills which would supply water to the town's residents until 1969 when East Providence would tie into the Providence water system.

Other public works projects followed the formation of the town's water department, but they were of a different nature. The public improvements of the 1930's were designed not simply to better living conditions in the community but essentially to put people back to work; for by 1930 the Great Depression had begun its decade-long dominance of American life.

It all began with the stock market crash in October 1929. The crash destroyed business confidence and wiped out many large and small investors. When these effects were combined with the fact that the long-term capital that the market supplied for business expansion was no longer available, an economic depression began in 1930 and intensified for the next several years while the Federal government attempted to come to grips with it. But the Great Depression would only end a decade later when America began to prepare for World War II, and as a result production for military purposes stimulated the economy and created jobs.

But prior to this the United States experienced unprecedented peacetime suffering which left deep scars on the American psyche. A twenty-five percent unemployment rate hung over the nation. Breadlines and shanty towns appeared in metropolitan areas.

In East Providence population statistics outlined the magnitude of the Depression. The town contained 29,995 residents at the start of the Depressison in 1930. Six years later the population had risen by only 118 people, where in the 1920's it had been increasing by over 900 a year!

The Federal government under Franklin D. Roosevelt instituted a number of programs to counter the despair which dominated the American nation. Efforts were concentrated on creating jobs. The government agreed to loan or grant cities and towns a portion of the money needed to finance public projects. Under this agreement, East Providence built a new reservoir and dam and made other improvements in its water supply system. The town also received money to remodel and enlarge its schools. Alterations were made on the Bliss Primary School and the Arthur E. Platt School, for example.

More important were the additions which the town built to the junior and senior high schools on Broadway. The latter, it will be recalled, was overcrowded from the time of its opening in 1910, and the continued expansion of East Providence's population in the post World War I years had brought about emergency measures. Beginning in 1919, no new pupils from Seekonk were accepted and in 1922 double sessions began in the high school. By 1926 officials had decided that junior high schools were needed to alleviate congestion in the high school by removing most of the freshman class.

In 1928 Central Junior High School opened to serve students from Watchemoket, Rumford and Phillipsdale, while Riverside still sent freshmen to the high school. Three years later, however, a grammar school in that section of town was enlarged and remodelled and Riverside Junior High School began receiving students. Finally, in 1933 under the New Deal's Public Works Administration, the town borrowed

The Platt House on Willett Avenue, on the site of John Brown's home

$171,430 to add twenty rooms to East Providence High School and Central Junior High School, thus providing, for a while at least, adequate classroom space for the town's student population.

An early postcard view of East Providence High School

Other public works projects were launched in the community under various New Deal agencies of the Federal government. Under the Works Progress Administration (W.P.A.), for instance, numerous new streets were laid out while others were rebuilt. Miles and miles of sidewalks were constructed all over town, and a large drainage system was built along Bourne Avenue.

Pierce Memorial Field was also a W.P.A. project. The site of the athletic field was an abandoned gravel pit which belonged to the McCormick Construction Company. For a number of years the gravel pit had gradually been developing into a public dump, breeding rats and foul odors and taking the honor of perhaps the biggest eyesore in East Providence. The town council managed to acquire the land in place of the taxes owed by its owner and received the approval of the W.P.A. to construct a football field. Workers were paid the Depression wage of 65 cents per hour, and the total cost of the projct was $300,000. The field was named after W. P. Pierce, a prominent resident of East Providence who had left a trust fund for recreational purposes in the town. Pierce

Pierce Memorial Field is one of the improvements dating back to W.P.A. projects of the Depression years

Memorial Field opened in 1938, just in time for the traditional football game between East Providence High School and La Salle Academy.

In addition to P.W.A. and W.P.A. sponsored projects, other privately funded civic improvements were completed in the 1930's. The Bradley Hospital and Weaver Memorial Library are two cases in point.

Bradley Hospital was built with money from the trust of Mr. and Mrs. George Lothrop Bradley who wanted to establish a memorial to their only daughter who had died as a young woman. Emma Pendleton Bradley, for whom the hospital was named, had suffered throughout her youth from a nervous disorder which doctors were able neither to diagnose nor cure. Her parents took her from doctor to doctor only to see her condition worsen until she died in young adulthood.

Mr. and Mrs. Bradley then decided that upon their death much of their estate would be set aside for the establishment of a home where children suffering emotional disorders similar to their daughter's could receive help. From the "misfortune of our only child," Bradley wrote in his will, "has grown the purpose and the hope that from the affliction of this one life may come comfort and blessing to many suffering in like manner."

After the death of the Bradleys, a board of trustees was formed to lay plans for the hospital. Thirty-five acres of farm land and woods

The entrance sign to Bradley Memorial Hospital is a reminder that it was one of the first, in 1931, to care for children with emotional disorders.

along Pawtucket Avenue in Riverside were purchased and workmen began constructing a large brick building and recreational facilities on the grounds.

In April 1931 the Emma Pendleton Bradley Home, the only hospital of the time in the United States dealing exclusively with children afflicted with emotional disorders, began receiving patients. Children were admitted without respect to race, nationality or religion, preference being given only to the needy and to residents of Rhode Island. From modest beginnings in 1931, the facilities and staff of the hospital, as well as the number of its patients, would continue to grow until the Bradley hospital would gain a nationwide reputation.

Like the Bradley Hospital, the Weaver Memorial Library was financed by a bequest. The benefactor was Mrs. Susan B. Anthony who financed the library to honor her mother, Mrs. Susan Weaver, one of the founders of the Watchemoket Free Library in the late nineteenth century. Mrs. Anthony's will set aside money and land belonging to the Weaver family for a new library. In 1938 the Weaver Memorial Library

Weaver Memorial Library, like Bradley Hospital, was donated to the community through a private bequest.

opened and was flanked by a small park (Weaver Memorial Park) and another building, the Weaver Welfare Memorial, both of which were also bequests of Mrs. Anthony.

Of all the public and private projects completed in East Providence in the 1930's, none aroused more enthusiasm and controversy than Narragansett Race Track. Within three years of its opening in 1934, armed camps were poised to battle for control of the contested territory around the track's perimeter. Although most of the race track was within the boundaries of the City of Pawtucket, a part of it overlapped into East Providence. Thus the story of the famous political fight to clean up the operation of the race track and the area surrounding it is part of the history of East Providence.

The stormy early years of Narragansett Race Track resemble the script of classic 1920's gangster movies. Cast in the role of the villain was Walter E. O'Hara, the founder and president of the race track.

Prior to opening the horse racing facility, O'Hara was a businessman in Fall River, Massachusetts. His principal interests were in textile mills, but he was also a part owner in tube and advertising companies in Boston. In addition he had joined other businessmen in the construction and operation of a race track in Houston, Texas.

In May of 1934, as the Depression continued to worsen in spite of the efforts of the Federal government, Rhode Islanders voted overwhelmingly (four to one) to establish pari-mutuel horse racing in the state. Two days later O'Hara founded the Narragansett Racing Association, and by the beginning of June a race track was under construction on Newport Avenue.

O'Hara had little difficulty securing the approval of the East Providence town council, but the politicians of the City of Pawtucket, from which the race track would receive most of its public services, proved to be obstinate. Thomas McCoy, for example, the leader of the Democratic party in Pawtucket, demanded that O'Hara hire a large number of his city's unemployed residents to build and work at the race track or else he would see to it that the facility's supply of water would be cut off and road and sewer improvements would not be made. O'Hara completed an agreement with McCoy, and the two powerful men became allies for the battles ahead.

Throughout the summer of 1934, O'Hara supervised the project, over 1,800 workers labored at a hectic pace and residents of Pawtucket and East Providence watched in amazement as the race track took shape almost overnight. Within seven weeks tons of dirt were moved, water and sewer pipes were laid, telephone and electric cables were installed, and the track, a grandstand and other buildings were completed.

On August 1, 1934 the 1.2 million dollar track – the most talked-about local event in Rhode Island that year – opened for business. "Rhode Island gave a thunderous welcome to the prodigal sport," the *Providence Journal* reported. A crowd estimated at over 37,000 bet in excess of $350,000 dollars on opening day. Both winners and losers agreed with the *Baltimore Sun* which wrote that Narragansett Race Track was "The showplace of the North, one of the finest tracks in the country."

But it would soon develop a more infamous reputation, until Governor Robert Quinn declared a state of insurrection existed in a one-mile area of Pawtucket and East Providence bordering on the race track, and took effective measures to put down the uprising. The trouble began simultaneously with the opening of the race track. Illegal "bookie" operations sprang up all over Rhode Island. It is said that the City of Pawtucket alone contained over 100 illegal gambling establishments. Later Governor Quinn charged that not only did the race track breed "bookies" but it also attracted thugs and gangsters. Moreover, the Governor would maintain in 1937, McCoy and O'Hara used money and political muscle to control politicians and when this did not work the owner of the race track brought in "known criminals to intimidate and coerce public officials."

The beginning of the end for O'Hara, if not for McCoy, began in 1936 when Quinn received the Democratic nomination for governor. O'Hara had supported McCoy in the primary not simply with money but also with his newspaper, the *Pawtucket Star Tribune.* On the other hand, the *Providence Journal* strongly opposed both O'Hara's operation of the race track and McCoy's political designs.

Consequently, several months after Quinn took office, O'Hara's henchmen attacked a *Journal* photographer and reporter. The Governor now decided that the long train of public abuses at and around the race track had to be challenged. He ordered O'Hara to appear before the State Racing Commission to show cause why he should not be denied the right to operate the race track. The commission concluded that O'Hara should be removed, but the state Supreme Court blocked the decision.

Governor Quinn then directed the racing commission to cancel the fall racing dates, but once again the Court intervened. In the midst of this maneuvering by both sides, Quinn was subjected to one of the most vituperative and libelous newspaper assaults in Rhode Island history. Almost daily O'Hara's *Star Tribune* spewed forth malicious stories slandering the Governor. On September 8, 1937, for example, the *Star Tribune* ran a front page headline which read: "Gov. Quinn Will Land in Butler's, O'Hara Says." (As everyone knew, Butler Hospital treated the mentally ill.) When the papers were folded for delivery the words "Will Land" and "O'Hara Says" were hidden from view and the headline seemed to read "Gov. Quinn in Butler's."

Quinn was now determined to block the opening of the track's fall racing season. He waited until October 16, two days before the track was to open, and drew up a proclamation which stated that an area of about three square miles surrounding the race track was in a state of insurrection. Martial law was declared, and several hundred National Guard soldiers, some of them armed with machine guns, were dispatched to the area and joined State Police in preventing the opening of the race track.

McCoy, now Mayor of Pawtucket, sent the city's police force to the race track in a show of arms that could have led to bloodshed. But the National Guard and State Police managed to keep control of the track grounds until November 11 when the racing season ended.

O'Hara's empire and political power began to crumble. He was ousted as president and manager of the race track by its stockholders. His newspaper went into receivership, and he was indicted (the charges were later dropped) for illegal contributions to the Democratic and Republican parties. Four years later O'Hara would be dead, the result of a head-on car crash on Route 44.

In spite of O'Hara's shenanigans, Narragansett Race Track was a major financial success in its early years. This is all the more remarkable when one considers that the state and the nation were still mired in the Depression. To be sure, the economy did recover somewhat between 1935 and 1937 when early New Deal spending began to take effect. But encouraged by this moderate upturn, the Roosevelt administration cut back funds for emergency programs. Consequently, the economy headed back downward in 1938, and the Depression was as bad if not worse than it had ever been.

For many Rhode Islanders the year 1938 brought further hardship.

The Narragansett Race Track was a popular attraction from the beginning, despite being the center of political controversies in the late 1930's.

The most powerful hurricane the state had ever felt ravaged both sides of Narragansett Bay.

With little advance warning the storm crashed into the Rhode Island coastline late in the afternoon of September 21. At five o'clock winds were clocked at 87 miles per hour, and, before the storm began to subside a few hours later, the hurricane's force would reach 121 miles per hour. Electric power and telephone service were knocked out. Homes along the shoreline were demolished, and everywhere trees were torn up by their roots. Downtown Providence was inundated by thirteen feet of water.

Roosevelt quietly began aiding France and Britain and preparing for

In East Providence the Riverside shoreline was particularly hard hit. Railroad tracks and docks were carried out to sea, and a huge oil tanker paid an unexpected visit to the grounds of the Squantum Club. Homes were washed across the upper Bay and deposited on the Riverside coast line. The Barrington Parkway was flooded, and at least two people who were attempting to cross it in vehicles were carried away by the rampaging water.

Over in Watchemoket the town's gasometer on First Street which contained 93,000 cubic feet of illuminating gas burst with a thunderous noise. At the town hall a short distance away, the chimney fell through the roof and fractured the skull of an East Providence policeman.

By early evening death and destruction were scattered all over Rhode Island. One hundred million dollars worth of damage and 300 fatalities, the final total would read. The task of clearing streets, railroad tracks and the incredible amount of debris which the storm had left in Narragansett Bay began the following day as National Guard troops stood by to prevent looting.

While the residents of Rhode Island would come to remember September of 1938 because of the hurricane, much of the rest of the world would recall it for another cataclysm. September was the month during which Adolf Hitler demanded that the Sudetenland in Czechoslovakia be handed over to Germany. At a hastily called and historic conference in Munich on September 24th, Great Britain and France yielded to Hitler who agreed to honor the remaining territorial sovereignty of Czechoslovakia. Within a matter of months, however, Hitler broke his Munich pledge and took over the entire country.

It became increasingly evident between 1939 and 1941 that if Western Europe fell the next target of Hitler would be the United States. war, and it was this military production, not New Deal programs, that ended the Depression. By December 7, 1941 when the Japanese attacked Pearl Harbor, unemployment was still rather high but the Depression was virtually over. The nearly four-year-long war that followed, however, further stimulated the economy and, with large numbers of men called into the service, unemployment gave way to a labor shortage.

East Providence joined big and small communities across the country in civilian efforts designed to support the war cause. Even before the Japanese attack on Pearl Harbor, the Federal government had begun establishing a national civil defense organization. Representatives of cities and towns from coast to coast gathered at the Army's Chemical Warfare School in Maryland in the fall of 1941 to learn the procedures for establishing local civil defense organizations. The representatives were also instructed in techniques for coping with chemical and gas warfare and for controlling the notorious incendiary bombs of the Germans.

From East Providence the town council sent Fire Chief Arthur A. Griswold and Police Chief James R. Crosby to the Chemical Warfare School. Upon their return to Rhode Island the two men organized the town's civil defense program. Auxiliary groups of firemen and policemen were formed to aid the regular forces if the community came under a bombing attack. Specialists in first aid were trained and rescue squads equipped with ambulances and trucks were established. All the divisions of the Civil Defense organization participated in air raid drills throughout the war.

The citizens of East Providence did not forget the well over two thousand young men and women from their community who were in uniform. A number of women in the town organized the East Providence Community Red Cross Surgical Dressing Unit. The group consisted of about 150 women who worked in shifts afternoons and evenings, five days a week, in the hall of the American Legion and in the town hall, turning out thousands of rolls of surgical dressings.

The East Providence veterans' organizations also made special efforts to support and show their appreciation for the town's armed forces. The Riverside Legion Post sent packages filled with items such as candy and razor blades to servicemen from that section of town while the Stark-Parker Post supplied similar tokens of appreciation to those from other areas of East Providence.

In the middle of the war, a Servicemen's Fund was established in East Providence, largely on the initiative of members of the Stark-Parker Post. Contribution boxes were placed in many stores throughout the town. Several businessmen followed the tack of Nick Karras, owner of the Alpha Spa on Warren Avenue, who, before returning change to a customer, would call his attention to the contribution box on the counter.

At the same time, the committee in charge of the Servicemen's Fund used newspaper advertising, church notices and even the loudspeakers on police cars to request families to send the names and addresses of their sons and husbands who were in uniform. Much information was communicated to the committee by Miss Mary Hill, the librarian at East Providence High School, who kept a scrapbook which listed the promotions and awards as well as the military stations of most of her former students. Miss Alice Waddington, another member of the high school faculty, wrote a local newsletter during the war which she sent to the town's fighting men around the world. In return, Miss Waddington received many moving letters.

The money which was raised by the Servicemen's Fund was spent for two items. First, arrangements were made with the Planters Nut and Chocolate Company to send each East Providence soldier a pound of nuts. Second, a better-than-twenty-page booklet which carried war news and good wishes from the town was printed and distributed to the servicemen.

The booklet was written, the authors informed their readers "like we would talk if we were together at the soda fountain at Arthur Allen's store or any other place." Each night it seemed, many members of the Servicemen's Fund committee met in the doorway of Ben Franklin's Store on Taunton Avenue to discuss the progress of the war and military events of the day. They jokingly dubbed themselves the "Civilian Board of Military Strategy."

By the summer of 1944 this group, along with all Americans, found a measure of hope as the allies appeared to be gaining the advantage in the war. The successful invasion of Normandy took place in June, and by October the Germans were no longer in France. As the Allies continued to push toward Germany from the west, the Russians approached from the east. By the spring of 1945 Germany was ready to surrender.

Now full attention could be paid to the Far East. On July 29th the Japanese were ordered to surrender or face "prompt and utter destruction." This ultimatum was rejected, and the first atomic bombs in history were dropped on Hiroshima and Nagasaki in early August. Less than a month later, the Japanese surrendered.

Communities across the country celebrated the end of one of the bloodiest wars in history and began to erect memorials to those who had lost their lives. Since 1942 in East Providence, high school students had been raising money for a memorial by collecting and selling waste paper. With this money, memorial gates were erected at Pierce Field in honor of the 2,125 former students of the high school who served in

The memorial gates at Pierce Field honor those who served in World War II, and were erected through fund-raising efforts of East Providence high school students.

The Barrington Parkway's name was changed to honor the soldiers of World War II.

the war, and the 76 who lost their lives. At about the same time the name of the Barrington Parkway was changed to the Veteran's Memorial Parkway.

As the veterans returned to East Providence and the postwar era opened, a major political battle began to take shape in the town. Bitter political warfare would rage in the town from shortly after the end of military hostilities to the late 1950's. But East Providence would emerge from the struggle unscathed, as its selection as an All-American City in 1958 would prove.

VIII
Transformation from Town to "All-American City"

From the time of East Providence's incorporation in 1862 to 1946, the Republican party monopolized elective and appointive town offices and held a determinative influence over town affairs. A more important measure of the political status quo in East Providence may be found in the fact that the town had grown from a population of 1,850 in 1862 to over 32,000 by the end of the war – the town budget had expanded just as dramatically – and yet, in spite of this dynamic growth, the town was still administered under the traditional New England town meeting system of government. Indeed, East Providence achieved notoriety as one of the largest, if not the largest, community in the United States to be run under the town meeting form of government.

In East Providence this political system, which among other things was a legacy of the Puritans and Pilgrims of the seventeenth century, was tinkered with down through the years but not substantially altered. An elected five-man council (except for the period 1863-1876 when the number of council members was reduced to three) administered the town until 1946. The council was elected every year until 1916, when two-year terms were introduced. The town council chose its own president, selected the town moderator and controlled a number of appointive positions.

But the real power of this five-man body derived from its right to make administrative and even some legislative decisions affecting town affairs. Financial authority, however, resided with the people, that is, with those eligible to vote. At the annual town meeting, over which the town moderator presided, appropriations and major legislative issues were voted on by those property owners present, usually far from a majority of eligible voters.

As town expenses grew and a dwindling percentage of an expanding population attended the yearly financial meeting, some sentiment for a change in East Providence's form of government surfaced. The inadequacy of the political system, and the desire for major alterations in it, were expressed as early as 1914. The following resolution was passed in the financial town meeting of that year:

> Whereas the half (sic) hazard method of making appropriations by the town meeting is not conducive to a sound financial policy for the town, and Whereas; it would be impossible for all voters to attend the meeting for want of a large enough hall in which to meet, Be it resolved; That a committee of twenty-five (25), Five (5) residents of each voting district be elected to consider various forms of municipal government now in use and to draft a charter suitable to the needs of East Providence.

This reform sentiment, however, did not realize its primary goal of changing the town's existing governmental structure.

It did, nonetheless, lead to an amendment of the town meeting form of government which attempted to bring a measure of efficiency and order to fiscal affairs. Beginning in 1916, fifteen taxpayers were chosen to serve as a Budget Committee with considerable authority over town expenditures. The town council, the school committee and individual departments of government were required to draw up detailed budgets which were submitted to the Budget Committee. This group of taxpayers then carefully examined each request, made any changes that were deemed necessary, and issued a report which recommended a budget for approval at the yearly financial town meeting.

The establishment of a Budget Committee certainly did not compensate for all of the deficiencies in the operation of the town meeting form of government in a large community like East Providence. It did at least appease those seeking moderate reform, and disarm more vocal critics – until, that is, a transformation in the political control of the town revived calls for a more efficient form of government.

After 84 years' status as political outsiders, the Democrats of East

Providence finally won representation on the town council in 1946. Two years later the Democrats gained control of the council and, with it, their long-desired domination of town government. This victory, like the rivalry between the two parties, was more than political, for the Democrats were largely Catholic ethnics, most notably the Irish and Portuguese, while the Republicans were, in the main, Protestant Anglo-Saxons. In short, the triumph of the Democrats in 1948 symbolized the emergence in the political sphere of a transformation in the social, religious and ethnic composition of the town, a change that had been going on since the late nineteenth century.

The Democrats, under the leadership of James J. Reilly, president of the town council (now increased to nine members), assumed management of the local government at an important point in the history of East Providence. During the postwar years the population of the town began to surge once again, and with it came a new demand for the extension of public services which could only be met by enlarging the town's budget.

New schools, for example, were a major financial burden throughout the late 1940's and 1950's. Overcrowding at the high school forced officials to borrow classrooms from Central Junior High School for the excess students. It became obvious by 1947 that a new high school was required. In addition, an expanding enrollment in the lower grades created the need for new elementary schools.

At the annual town meeting in November of 1947, the school committee introduced a resolution requesting $55,000 to purchase thirty acres of land on Pawtucket Avenue where a new high school would be built. A second resolution asking for $20,000 to begin planning for the structure was also presented. After initial approval, a second town meeting rejected the purchase money and instead passed a resolution to have the Town Moderator appoint a non-partisan committee of taxpayers to work with the school committee, investigating sites for the high school and making recommendations. Finally, the original 30-acre tract was purchased for $60,000.

It now remained for the proponents of improved educational facilities to convince East Providence voters to approve several million dollars in bond issues to construct the high school and two elementary schools. In the months preceding the town meeting in November of 1949, when the crucial vote was to be taken, school officials, teachers, the P.T.A. and even students joined in a well organized campaign to convince voters that the future of East Providence depended upon the approval of money for the new school buildings.

The efforts of these groups were successful, for the town meeting authorized officials to raise the required sum of money. Construction began in the summer of 1950 and two years later the Carl T. Thompson and the James R. D. Oldham elementary schools were completed. In the same year, an ultra-modern high school building was opened. The *Providence Journal* later reported that the facility was "considered by educators as one of the finest high schools in the country."

East Providence High School, completed in 1952, was one of the first modern high schools in the country.

The three buildings completed in 1952 marked the beginning of a wave of school construction unprecedented in the history of East Providence. In addition to the high school and the Oldham and Thompson schools, the town council sought and won approval for these schools built in the 1950's: the Waddington, the Watters, the Hennesey, the Whitenact and the Grove Avenue. In 1951, early in this period of dynamic growth for the East Providence school system, Edward R. Martin was appointed superintendent.

Beyond providing for the educational needs of a rapidly expanding population, the town was confronted with another expensive problem — the glaring inadequacy of the town's sewer system. Most areas of East Providence were without sewers. The exception was Watchemoket which had created its own sewer district and had begun its own system in 1905. For the other areas, a small treatment plant built in 1928 was unable to meet standards set by the State Health Department.

In 1947 a town Sewer Committee was appointed, and it issued a report the following year. "To protect the health of our citizens, to attract new enterprises and to gain new residents," the committee concluded, "it would seem part of wisdom and good judgment to at least make a start toward a comprehensive sewer system."

By 1951, with money from general tax revenues and bond issues, the construction of a modern sewer system in East Providence was in full progress. Miles of trunk lines and drains were laid, and in 1953 the new Pomham Treatment Plant began operating. The sewer system stimulated the industrial and residential growth of the town. Manufacturers in particular were no longer discouraged from locating in East Providence, as they had been for years, because of the unavailability of sewers.

New sewers and schools, as well as other civic advances (improvements in the town's water supply system, for example) which the town council supported, required heavy capital expenditures. This financial reality prompted town officials to launch a program of property reevaluation. Needless to say, reevaluation aroused considerable opposition from the voters, and fueled the campaign of those who had been seeking government reform in East Providence for several years.

Calls for major political change began in 1948, the same year that the Democrats came to power. The League of Women Voters initiated a study of East Providence's government, and released a report in 1948 which maintained that there was widespread inefficiency, waste and political patronage in the operation of the town. The following year the League concluded that East Providence should be rechartered as a city and began to investigate alternatives to the town meeting form of government. A booklet entiled "Which Way East Providence" was published and described various types of city government, with the city manager form getting the League's endorsement.

This was the start of a drive to streamline local government which would culminate nearly a decade later in a new city charter. The interplay of several factors accounted for the rise and ultimate success of reform. First, an expanding population and rising town expenses convinced many people during the postwar years that East Providence had outgrown the town meeting form of government. By 1950 the population of East Providence was almost 36,000. Of this number 15,000 were eligible to vote, but on the average only 300 voters (or 2%) attended the annual financial town meeting.

Another factor contributing to the movement for reform was a shift in the balance of power exemplified by the victory of the Democrats with their largely Catholic constituency. A similar shift occurred in a number of other Rhode Island communities – Pawtucket and Newport, for example – and prodded Republicans and Independents to lead campaigns for political reform throughout the state in the 1950's.

Other issues also fed the fires of reform in East Providence. Reevaluation certainly played a role, as did the feeling on the part of some Democrats that their party was not distributing the spoils of office evenly.

The movement for reform began to gain momentum with the formation of a Citizens League. Since the League of Women Voters, the first group to advocate change in East Providence, was forbidden by its charter from direct involvement in partisan politics, members formed a separate group to work for reform through political channels. Organized in 1951, the Citizens League of East Providence held its first official meeting on March 4, 1952 and elected Robert E. Lee of Rumford president.

From its founding, the League's major goal was to secure a new charter for the town. All who supported this objective, whether they were Democrats, Republicans or Independents, were invited to join the League. During its first year of existence membership reached 600 and, as the League increasingly thrust itself into the eye of one of the largest political storms in modern Rhode Island history, its support expanded commensurately.

In addition to the founding of the Citizens League, 1951 was a critical time in the brewing controversy for another reason. That same year Rhode Island voters approved a Home Rule Amendment to the State Constitution which gave cities and towns the authority to decide for themselves, without the sanction of the General Assembly, what type of local government they wanted. Thus, under this amendment a charter commission was elected in December of 1951 to recommend a new form of government to the voters of East Providence. Four of the nine positions on the commission went to members of the League of Women Voters who voted for a city manager government. However, a majority favored a strong mayor government, and a charter providing for a change to that form was presented to the voters.

The leadership of the Democratic Party supported the position of the charter commission majority, but the electorate did not. In 1952 the voters rejected the strong mayor charter, and the Citizens League began a new drive which it hoped would culminate in city manager government.

First, members of the League went from door to door and gathered approximately 3,000 signatures, well over the number needed to call an election for a new charter commission. Once this was accomplished the League decided to run its own candidates for the charter commission so that opponents of the city manager form of government would not get a majority of the nine seats on the commission. The League's candidates and hundreds of volunteers canvassed neighborhoods and distributed leaflets explaining what was at stake in the upcoming election. Their efforts paid off handsomely. In 1953 the Citizens League won eight of the nine berths on the charter commission.

After a year of investigation and discussion, the charter commission voted 8 to 1 for a council manger form of government. Having come this far, and apparently on the verge of victory, the Citizens League took precautions to blunt an expected counterattack by the political foes of the new charter. An energetic public education campaign was conducted throughout 1954. A 40-member speakers' bureau was organized which delivered nearly 100 addresses to civic, religious and fraternal groups in East Providence. Countless circulars explaining the city manager charter were distributed by the Citizens League and the League of Women Voters.

On the other hand, opponents of the new charter mobilized for a forceful counteroffensive. The charter was unacceptable to many political leaders, Democrats and Republicans alike, for a number of reasons. Since the charter called for off-year, non-partisan elections, they argued that the two-party system in East Providence would be destroyed. Furthermore, they pointed out that off-year elections were not likely to encourage a large turnout of voters. Therefore, the possibility of a well organized minority controlling elections was enhanced. Finally, many political opponents of the Citizens League felt, as one of them put it,

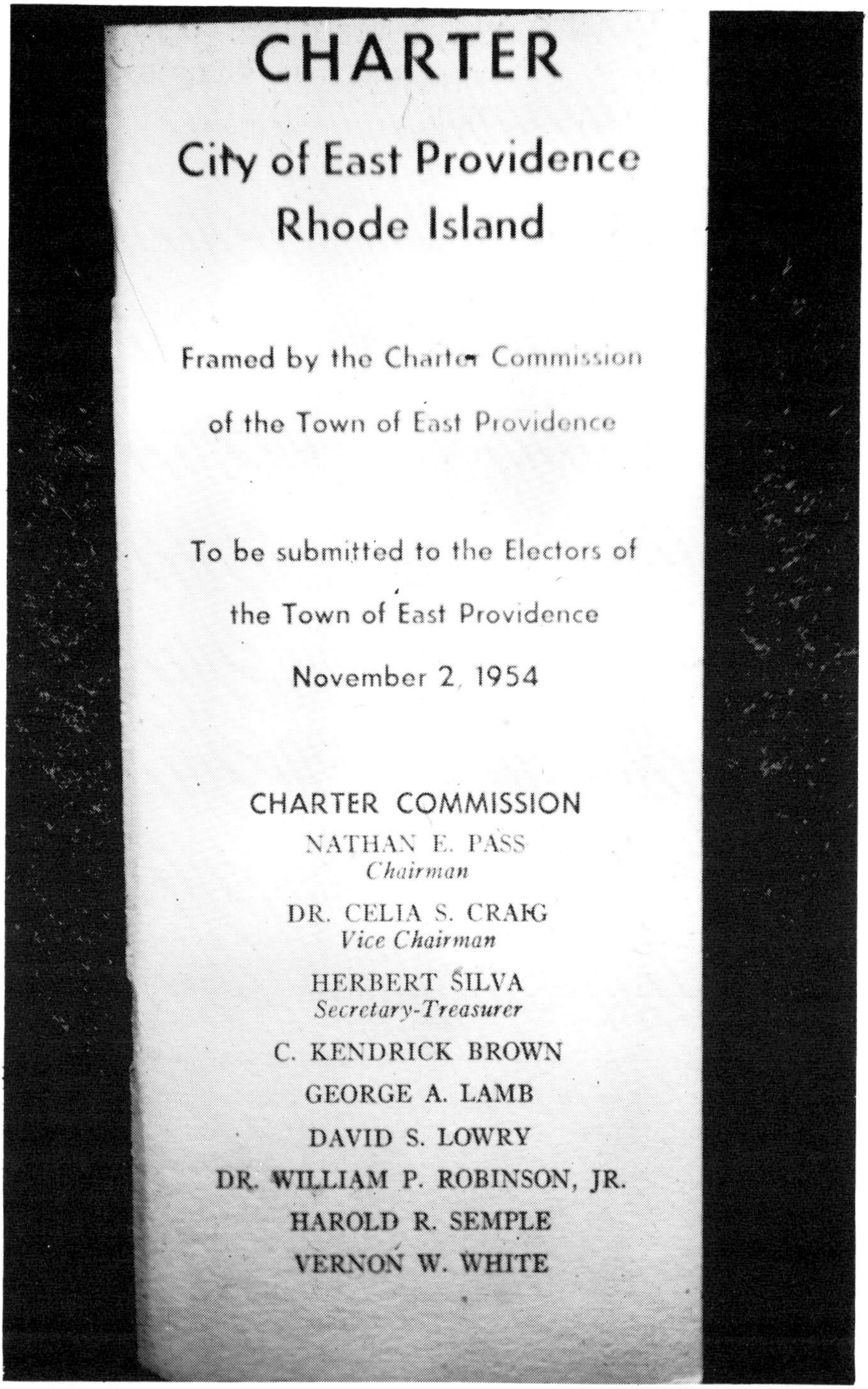

CHARTER

City of East Providence
Rhode Island

Framed by the Charter Commission

of the Town of East Providence

To be submitted to the Electors of

the Town of East Providence

November 2, 1954

CHARTER COMMISSION

NATHAN E. PASS
Chairman

DR. CELIA S. CRAIG
Vice Chairman

HERBERT SILVA
Secretary-Treasurer

C. KENDRICK BROWN

GEORGE A. LAMB

DAVID S. LOWRY

DR. WILLIAM P. ROBINSON, JR.

HAROLD R. SEMPLE

VERNON W. WHITE

Years of community effort won this charter and the reform of local government.

that the people of East Providence "didn't know many of the provisions in the charter."

These criticisms were not accepted by a majority of those who voted in the charter election of 1954. A record 85% of the electorate cast ballots and the charter was approved by a 9,288 to 7,884 vote. In spite of this result, the victory was not yet in hand; instead, the life of the town meeting form of government was prolonged for three more years. This unforeseen turn of events resulted from the fact that the Home Rule Amendment did not grant local communities the power to change election provisions without the approval of the state legislature. The members of that body were reluctant to act on a charter which could potentially undermine the two-party system in an important and growing community like East Providence.

In 1955 the Citizens League and the League of Women Voters decided to carry their reform drive to the General Assembly. A bill authorizing the charter was introduced, and it was sent to the Senate Corporation Committee for study. Representatives of the Citizens League and the League of Women Voters appeared before the committee and urged approval of the bill. Lobby groups were organized to put pressure on state officials. But the 1955 session of the General Assembly ended with the legislation still stalled in committee. As State Senator William J. Smith of Warren, Chairman of the Corporation Committee, reported, "Neither party wanted that bill."

The East Providence Town Council then tried another approach. It requested Attorney General William Powers to decide whether the provisions of the charter which did not relate to elections could be implemented. The Attorney General delayed judgment and then ruled that "no part of the Charter could take effect until the General Assembly validated the election machinery."

Following this decision, State Senator Joseph R. Weisberger of East Providence introduced and managed Senate passage of a resolution which asked the Supreme Court for an opinion (never rendered) on the Attorney General's ruling. Governor Dennis J. Roberts also became involved at this time and urged that the General Assembly "should at the earliest possible time make certain that the East Providence charter becomes operative so that the community may enjoy the fruits of self government."

Early in 1956 the Citizens League returned to the fray armed with new tactics. On St. Valentine's Day cards which combined appropriate greetings with political barbs were sent to the lawmakers. "Love and government are games of barter, here's our heart, where's our charter," read one card. "Here comes Cupid wreathed in smiles, to pry our Bill from Committee files," offered another.

To make sure the politicians interpreted these messages clearly, one hundred members of the Citizens League and League of Women Voters marched on the State House to voice their disgust with the inaction of the General Assembly. Another delegation of 50 returned the next month. Still in spite of this public outcry and the growing embarrassment of public officials, the charter bill remained buried beneath a mound of political calculations.

Finally, in the midst of mounting public pressure and indignation, the General Assembly was forced into action. In April of 1957, almost two and one-half years after the voters of East Providence had approved the city manager charter, the state legislature produced a validation bill. But the legislation had two catches.

First, the General Assembly made the bill a referendum issue which would have to be put to another town-wide vote. Second, the questions which composed the validation bill were written so that if a person approved all the provisions of the new charter he would have to vote no to each item! The result was East Providence's famous "upside down" election.

Again, the Citizens League and the League of Women Voters set in motion a campaign to clarify the issues for the voters of the town. Literature informing people how to vote correctly was made available in all sections of East Providence. Volunteers pounded pavements from Riverside to Rumford. The electorate responded by approving the same charter for the second time in three years. Soon East Providence would be reclassified as a city and would be run by an appointed city manager.

The charter changed several election procedures. The council which was increased to nine members in 1946 was cut to five. Voting districts were reduced to four renamed wards, electing one councilor each. The fifth member of the city council was elected at large.

The members of the Citizens League reasoned that if the new charter was to work it required a council which supported it. For this reason, the League nominated its own candidates for the five city council positions. Over five hundred volunteers worked on behalf of these candidates. Suppers and raffles were organized to raise funds. In the first municipal election in November of 1958, Samuel H. Ramsay and

Stephen Walsh, two office seekers backed by the League, were elected to the city council. Shortly after the election a Democrat, Charles A. Reilly, became an ally of the League councilors and formed a majority determined to select a qualified city manager and set the new government off on the right foot.

The operation of municipal affairs under the new charter was uncomplicated. The city council was essentially a legislative body whose chief duties included the right to appoint and remove the city manager, to issue bonds and to oversee, and if necessary investigate, the work of all municipal departments. The council also elected one of its members mayor. Daniel Marso, the city's first mayor, held no administrative responsibilities and his principal duty was simply to preside over city council meetings.

The chief administrator, of course, was the city manager. He supervised the operation of municipal departments and held the authority to hire and fire city employees. He was also responsible for preparing the budget.

In addition to these changes in the structure of government, the charter contained provisions designed to neutralize political influence. City employees were not allowed to have private financial dealings with the municipal government. Dual office holding was prohibited and all city boards were required to be bipartisan in composition. Moreover, the records of all city businesses were to be available to the public.

The new government was not completely organized and the charter reform did not take full effect until a city manager took office. Following the council election of November 1958, an exhaustive search was conducted for a city manager. After interviewing numerous candidates the city council elected Earl P. Sandquist, at the time city manager of Aurora, Colorado (a suburb of Denver), to become East Providence's new chief executive.

Sandquist took over the city manager's job on May 1, 1959 as the Providence *Evening Bulletin* warned that his performance "will be watched with interest throughout the State of Rhode Island." Critics of the new charter were bound to latch onto any of Sandquist's errors to discredit the entire reform movement which had led to the establishment of the new government. The *Evening Bulletin* accurately pointed out what was at stake in East Providence: "The import Mr. Sandquist's reign engenders could easily determine the pace, and even fate, of the home rule movement in Rhode Island. His administration will provide food for thought for home rule enthusiasts, if it is given a fair chance and is successful; if the contrary prevails, political partisans will have a field day—for a long time."

Six months after the arrival of Sandquist the consensus seemed to be that East Providence was on the threshold of a new era. During this period the city manager had prepared and sent to the city council a budget which provided for a thorough reorganization of city government, for much-needed improvements in the operations of city departments, and for the present and future financial stability of the city. Many residents of the city agreed with the assessment made by former town council president James J. Reilly. "I've looked at 14 municipal budgets," he stated, "and Mr. Sandquist's is the finest this community has had in 14 years."

All of the reforms which the budget proposed and which were instituted in the first two years of the new council manager government are too numerous to list. Some of the more important improvements were: the reorganization of the finance and public works departments; the creation of a central purchasing department with competitive bidding rules; the establishment of an engineering division and a planning department; the development of a sanitary landfill and reclamation program. Furthermore, city money was appropriated for a five-room school addition, for public works equipment, for improvements in the water system and for a 10 percent increase in the salaries of municipal employees. Yet in spite of all these accomplishments and expenditures, the tax rate was actually reduced along with the city's bonded indebtedness.

As the early successes of the council manager government became evident by late 1960, civic leaders decided to apply to the yearly "All-American City" competition of the National Municipal League. In reality East Providence was reapplying for the award, because the original application was submitted in 1955 while the charter controversy was still raging. At that time officials of the National Municipal League informed the leaders of the Citizens League and League of Women Voters that it would be more appropriate for East Providence to enter the competition once the charter government was in operation. It was on the basis of this recommendation that Mrs. R. Gale Noyes, secretary of the Citizens League, filed a new application in 1960.

The "All-American City" competition was designed to afford recognition to communities across the nation that had through local efforts managed to accomplish progressive change. Applications were screened by a committee, finalists were selected and representatives of these cities and towns were invited to present their cases before National Municipal League officials. Finally, eleven All-American City awards would be conferred.

East Providence joined 102 other communities in competing for the honors. The entries ranged from the small town of Arkansas City, whose population was less than 1,000, to the big city of Baltimore with nearly one million residents. In the fall of 1960 East Providence was chosen one of the twenty-two finalists in the competition.

In November Stephen Walsh, a Citizens League city councilman as well as a lawyer and professor of business administration at Providence College, was chosen to recount East Providence's reform efforts before the National Conference on Government to be held later that month in Phoenix, Arizona. Expectations ran high in the community, for residents justifiably believed that they had a strong case.

"Immediately after the close of World War II," Walsh began his address to the National Conference on Government, "the Town of East Providence lay like a slumbering giant." He went on to describe the outdated governmental structure of the town, the beginning of the drive for reform, the actions of political opponents, the perseverance of the Citizens League and the ultimate election victory and success of the council-manager charter. In short, Walsh concluded his presentation: political reform was achieved in the city "as a result of the efforts of a few who initiated the campaign for home rule as far back as 1948, and whose forces expanded throughout the succeeding years to a point where thousands of citizens joined in the movement for good government in East Providence."

Although official announcement of the judges' decision was not expected until mid-march of 1961, residents of the city began to receive strong indications that East Providence had been chosen an All-American City. In December photographers from *Look* magazine, which sponsored the competition in concert with the National Municipal League, visited the community. For the next few months, rumors to the effect that East Providence had indeed attained All-American City status circulated throughout town. Finally, on March 16, 1961, the awards "for vigorous citizen action in bringing about major civic improvements" were announced and East Providence was on the select list of eleven.

Plans were immediately begun to celebrate the national recognition which the city had won. Throughout the spring residents hailed the rebirth of civic pride and good government in East Providence. On April 6, an award dinner at Crescent Park was attended by nearly 500 people. The main speaker, Harold H. Webber, an executive of *Look* magazine, congratulated the citizens for their achievements and officially presented the award to Mayor Marso.

Other festivities followed later that spring. On May 4th, Rhode Island Independence Day, there was a huge parade. This was followed by a city-wide cleanup program which attempted to capitalize on and extend East Providence's newfound self-esteem. "All-American City" decals and banners appeared on cars and store windows all over the community.

Less than a year later, as the glory of their recent accomplishments began to fade, the residents of East Providence had their civic pride rekindled by the city's centennial celebration. March 1, 1962 marked exactly 100 years of the city's history. Again, an official commemorative program was planned.

On March 1st, a state proclamation was issued declaring the occasion "East Providence Day." The theme of the official celebration was "A Century of Development," and the following month businesses, civic organizations and municipal departments held a week-long exposition at the high school with displays designed to show change during the first hundred years of the city's history. Other events included the selection of a Centennial Queen, a ball at Crescent Park, and a parade.

In addition, essay contests revolving around the Centennial theme were held in all public and private schools in the city. First prize, a $1,000 savings bond, was won by a student at East Providence High School. The winning essay contrasted life in East Providence when the community of 1,850 inhabitants was incorporated in 1862, with life in the city of approximately 43,000 in 1962. The essay asked rhetorically, "What is East Providence doing in the modern world? Does it keep pace with the times?" The author's response, after surveying 100 years of history, was unequivocal. "The answer," the student said, "must be an unqualified yes!"

But it would seem a more objective reading of the city's history, of American history for that matter, would indeed require a qualified answer. As the charter controversy demonstrated, "keeping pace with the times" was often achieved in a "crab-like manner" – that is, by moving sidewards in a zigzag fashion in order to move forward. In retrospect, and bearing in mind the facts of the charter fight, or the evolution of the school system (particularly the high school), or the establishment of a modern sewer system, the first 100 years of East Providence's history could be summed up this way: it was a period of remarkable growth in which public institutions and officials were constantly trying, in crab-like fashion, to "keep pace with the times."

As the charter – the crowning achievement of the first 100 years – demonstrated, progress may have been slow and halting in coming, but it was realized.

IX
The Second Hundred Years Begin, 1962-1975

The new council-manager government was established at a crucial time in East Providence's history. The charter took effect in 1958, almost exactly half way through the city's, indeed America's, prosperous post-World War II era (1945-70). The new form of government placed East Providence on solid political footing to deal with the immense problems which confronted the community and all of America during and beyond the 1960's.

Most of these problems – at least until the early 1970's when issues of ecology, economic recession, inflation, energy shortages and financial retrenchment by the Federal government marked a shift to new concerns and the end of the post-World War II era of dynamic growth – stemmed from the expansion of the population, or more precisely from the maturing of the generation which came into the world as part of the post-1945 baby boom. From a population of nearly 36,000 in 1950, East Providence grew to almost 42,000 in 1960, and then to 48,207 by 1970, making it the fifth largest city in the State of Rhode Island.

Only a part of East Providence's population growth during these years is attributable to a high birth rate. The other part may be traced to a second post-World War II trend–the flight to the suburbs. Old industrial cities like Pawtucket, Woonsocket and Providence lost large numbers of their inhabitants during these years. The population of Providence, for example, declined by over 41,000 between 1950 and 1960, and many of these residents migrated to suburban communities like East Providence, Cranston and Warwick.

Thus, through a high birth rate and migration the population of East Providence swelled, and taxed the ability of officials to provide municipal services for their new citizens. A particular burden was placed upon the school system. In 1963 the school department issued its first *Master Plan for Schools* which outlined a major building program:

School Construction

a) New Meadowcrest School
b) New Riverside Junior High School
c) New Orlo Avenue School
d) New Silver Spring School
e) Addition to Alice M. Waddington School
f) Addition to James R. D. Oldham School
g) New "Wampanoag Area" School

To finance the new construction, voters approved a large bond issue in 1966, and before the end of the decade almost the entire building program had become a reality. Along the way numerous jobs were created for construction trades workers and teaching opportunities abounded in the school system. All of this sharply contrasted with what would become the norm of the early 1970's.

In 1969 school officials issued a second report which amended the original *Master Plan,* and demonstrated new population trends in the city. A decline in births had begun in the early 1960's, and by the end of the decade the birth rate in East Providence was at the lowest point it had been in over twenty years. This was a national, not simply a local, phenomenon with far-reaching social and economic implications.

Further complicating the plans of East Providence school officials was the fate of the city's parochial schools. Throughout the 1960's rising costs which stemmed from inflation and the need to replace religious teachers with lay people undermined the financial stability of the city's parochial schools. As tuition rose, Catholic school population declined. Indeed, between 1960 and 1969, while East Providence's public school enrollment increased by 2,400, its parochial schools lost nearly 500 students.

The experience of St. Francis Xavier School was duplicated in other parts of the city. After long years of hard work and false starts, the Portuguese community of East Providence finally had its dream come true when the beautiful St. Francis School was completed in 1959. But the school's student population decreased by almost 21 percent in the

1960's. By 1969 the 7th and 8th grades were closed, and within a few years the building was transformed into a public school. Similar changes forced the closing of Our Lady of Loreto School at the same time. The need to revise post-World War II constant growth beliefs in the light of the reality of the late 1960's was suggested in the *School Plan* of 1969: "It appears that the construction of new parochial schools, or additions to present schools as anticipated in the 1963 *Master Plan for Schools*, are no longer appropriate assumptions."

Paralleling the decline in school construction was a dramatic downturn in the post-World War II housing boom. The flight to the suburbs had created a need not only for schools but for homes. Like school construction, home building contributed to the prosperity of the 1950's and 1960's by providing jobs for carpenters, plumbers, electricians and other tradesmen.

The identity of East Providence as primarily a residential community of the single family homes was already well established by the post-World War II years when a new wave of construction began. Many homes were built in the northern area of the city on land which formerly belonged to the Rumford Chemical Works. The south and south central areas of the city, from Route 195 to Riverside, experienced the city's largest residential growth in the 1960's. As one observer reported at this time, "Kent Heights and the streets off Willett Ave. in Riverside have hundreds of new homes."

The housing boom in East Providence took a new turn in the late 1960's. By that time many members of the post-World War II generation had attained young adulthood and had begun to marry. But this highly educated generation which had only known prosperity increasingly decided not to have children, or to postpone raising a family (usually a planned family of not more than one or two children) while the husband and wife worked, and both enjoyed and contributed to the prosperity of the 1960's. In short, a new young subculture of affluence emerged with the apartment complex and two cars for each unit its reigning symbols to compete with more traditional symbols of affluence – the ranch house in the suburbs with two cars in the driveway and a color television antenna on the roof.

The sudden explosion of apartment complexes in East Providence during the late 1960's is suggested by Planning Department statistics. Between 1960 and 1965, when single dwelling houses dominated the residential construction market, an average of 140 units per year were built in the city. From 1965 to 1973, however, an average of 380 units a year were added to the housing market in East Providence. Many of the apartment developments accounting for the rise were built in the Riverside area.

East Providence's share in the prosperity of the 1960's may be measured another way. It must be remembered that while the city is primarily a residential community, it is also a manufacturing center. Indeed, the term residential and manufacturing suburb best describes East Providence, and while the former sector of the community was expanding in the post-World War II years, so was the latter.

As we have seen, industrial growth throughout East Providence's history has been encouraged by the strategic location and natural advantages of the city. Several miles of coastline, excellent port facilities, particularly in Riverside, and access by rail lines or highways to all parts of the heavily populated southeastern New England area have made East Providence an attractive location for manufacturing and commercial industries.

By the early 1970's no less than 137 manufacturing firms were employing over 6,000 people in East Providence. The bulk of the city's industry revolved around the manufacturing of metals, machinery and jewelry, with the last being the single largest employer in East Providence. Other companies – manufacturers of textiles, paper products and chemicals, for example – brought industrial diversity to the city.

The world headquarters of Fram Corporation are located on Pawtucket Avenue in East Providence. In the same complex are a manufacturing facility and the world's most complete automotive filter engineering and research facility.

The Red Bridge, an historic old link between East Providence and Providence, was replaced by the Henderson Bridge at the end of the 1960's.

Then, too, East Providence continued to be the site of New England's only steel mill, Washburn Wire Company, and the location of the only refinery in the region, until it closed in 1974, to produce finished products from crude oil.

For a good part of its history East Providence has been a transportation crossroads, and two important highway improvements in the 1960's reinforced this tradition. First, in 1960 Interstate 195 opened. This major east-west artery was cut right through the center of East Providence, causing traffic problems for several years, but ultimately enhancing the city's position as a transportation intersection. By the end of the decade, the old Red Bridge, overburdened with the heavy flow of cars and trucks going to and from Providence and the scene of many traffic jams, was replaced by a modern structure, the Henderson Bridge.

Thus, the proximity of East Providence to superb highways and the location of the city in the heart of southeastern New England brought trucking firms and wholesale distributors to the city in the 1960's. East Providence boasted seven major trucking companies by 1970, and central warehouses were established in the city (those of the Cherry and Webb and Outlet companies, for instance) which distributed goods to units in chain stores throughout the area.

The impressive growth of transportation and distributing firms, and of manufacturing in the 1960's was surpassed by the expansion of East Providence's commercial economy. Since its earliest history, as we have seen, East Providence has existed as a cluster of distinct and virtually self-sufficient villages. From the days when each section of the city contained its own general store, blacksmith and cooper down to the present time, the commercial economy of East Providence has been decentralized, although Watchemoket did lay claim to commercial supremacy for several decades in the late nineteenth and early twentieth centuries.

During the 1960's and early 1970's, regional shopping centers appeared in various parts of the city, continuing East Providence's tradition of commercial decentralization. Gansett Plaza on Newport Avenue and Shopperstown and Wampanoag Mall at the busy intersection of Taunton and Pawtucket Avenues were the major commercial developments, with smaller retail blocks opening in other parts of the city.

Wampanoag Mall is a commercial development that retains the name of the Indian tribe that played so great a part in the area's colonial history.

As a result of this commercial expansion throughout the 1960's, retail sales in East Providence increased faster than in any other city in the State of Rhode Island, with the exception of Warwick where two huge malls were located. In terms of the sheer volume of retail sales,

East Providence was exceeded only by Warwick, Providence and Pawtucket, three considerably larger communities.

The dynamic industrial and commerçial growth of East Providence in the 1960's gave the city a third place ranking in the state, behind Warwick and Providence, in the total amount of manufacturing and retail construction. This expansion, along with tremendous residential growth, put new burdens on municipal officials who once more in the history of East Providence were forced to try to keep pace with rapid changes in their community. But now the city had a streamlined government, capable of handling new problems effectively.

In addition to enlarging and improving the school system to accommodate a swelling student population, East Providence officials, with the support of the electorate, initiated a number of civic improvements and programs between 1962 and 1975 which were designed in one way or another to preserve and better the quality of life in the community.

The creation of a new water supply system is a case in point. In 1964 East Providence voters approved a 7-million dollar bond issue so that the city could tie into Providence's excellent water supply system and improve existing mains and distribution facilities. The project was completed in 1969, and residents no longer had to use the inferior quality water from the Turner Reservoir. Furthermore, water lines were extended in all parts of the city so that by the early 1970's nearly 100 percent of the developed area of East Providence had water service.

Modern roadways flow under historic old stone overpasses and train trestles, as here on Roger Williams Avenue.

After upgrading the city's water system, officials turned their attention to the problem of sewage. Voters approved another bond issue of 1.5 million dollars to expand the city's Pomham Terrace Sewage Treatment Plant. When completed, this project will enable officials to extend sewers to all developed areas in East Providence.

A third field of civic advancement was community renewal. Riverside Square and Bullocks Point rehabilitation and renewal districts were established in the southern part of the city, for example, "to improve poor physical, social and environmental conditions" in the old resort area. Unfortunately, the drying up of Federal funds prevented implementation of renewal plans.

All of these programs required the cooperation of the Planning Department. And although it was only a few years old, having been established in the early months of City Manager Earl Sandquist's tenure, it became one of the busiest municipal departments in East Providence by the mid-1960's. From that period to 1975 the Department issued no less than 14 volumes of reports on all aspects of life in the city, ranging from housing to traffic and the economy.

The Planning Department's most recent report on land use suggests that the industrial, commercial and residential growth of East Providence in the 1960's and early 1970's may have brought the city to a development saturation point. The major finding of the survey was that only 14.3 percent of the total amount of land in East Providence remains undeveloped. "Much of this land," the report points out, "consists of small, scattered parcels with larger undeveloped parcels existing along the eastern boundary of the city." Furthermore, development of many of the larger areas of vacant land appears to be "hampered by the existence of wetlands, flooding conditions or excessively steep slope."

Given these facts, then, what does the future hold in store for East Providence? Trying to anticipate tomorrow is a hazardous business, as public officials throughout East Providence's history came to realize. But a few conclusions about the future seem reasonably certain.

In the first place the median educational attainment of the city's residents, which rose from 10.7 years in 1960 to 11.8 years in 1970, giving East Providence a ranking of fourth among Rhode Island cities (excluding towns), should continue to rise. Similarly, median family income which increased from $6,082 in 1960 to $10,179 in 1970 (third highest of all Rhode Island cities) should also continue to climb, not only as part of an inflationary spiral but also in terms of real income.

The alarm sounded at 2 a.m., January 12th. City Hall, a landmark in the center of the city since 1889, was in flames. Despite the efforts of firemen in the midst of a snowstorm, the City Hall and adjoining police station were gutted.

City Hall as it looked after the fire was extinguished

But the city will perhaps never again experience the dynamic growth which occurred in the late nineteenth and early twentieth centuries and particularly in the post-World War II era. It is doubtful that the projected population figure of 54,600 for the city in 1980 will be reached. It would also seem that the current residential-industrial balance in East Providence will not be substantially altered in the near future. That is, the city will remain essentially a residential suburb with homes and apartments occupying about 40 percent of the land in the community.

There will be unforeseen problems. A recent, spectacular example of this was the destruction of City Hall by fire last January 12th. Despite the efforts of firemen in the midst of a snowstorm, the building and adjoining police station were gutted. The state fire marshal's office later confirmed the assumption that faulty wiring caused the fire. There was not a major loss of valuable records, however, and the city government promptly continued to function from the new city garage and from wherever else space could be found.

In terms of the kinds of problems that can be anticipated, however, it seems clear that concern for the quality of community life will replace the older problems of quantitative growth. One such issue, the transformation of Turner Reservoir, the city's former source of water, into a municipal recreation area, is bound to come under serious consideration in the near future. A public recreation area of this sort would certainly add to the appeal of the city. But such quality of life improvements in East Providence are likely to run counter to another trend of the future – continuing financial retrenchment as a reaction to the most serious national economic slump since the Depression.

As the city and nation move to the close of the Bicentennial year, economic problems should not be allowed to cast a pall over the commemoration of two hundred years of the nation's history. They should, should, instead, help officials to use the Bicentennial to bring about a chastened understanding of America's revolutionary tradition, and not simply an emotional reaffirmation of it.

Epilogue:
The Bicentennial Celebration

In 1973 the East Providence City Council appointed a 13-member committee to plan Bicentennial programs for the community, one member for each of the original states. The members are Walter R. Martin, Chairman; Charles H. O'Connell, Vice Chairman and Treasurer; Eugene A. Amaral; Milton P. Blackwell; Claire M. Clegg; Robert L. Deasy; Harold N. Flint; Martha J. Gardner; Mary D. Irons; Katherine P. Rodman; Lotys R. Schanel; Elaine A. Silva and George R. Thompson.

For over two years now, the East Providence Bicentennial Committee has worked toward a renewed understanding of the ideals embodied in our nation's history, and a rededication to these ideals. The varied activities sponsored by the Committee in cooperation with city officials clearly reflect these twin goals.

During the spring of 1975, for example, the Committee conducted essay contests in the city's schools, organized a Bicentennial parade, planted a "liberty tree," and dedicated a small park at Fort Hill, the site of the city's Revolutionary War fortification. Other projects of the group include: the marking of graves of Revolutionary War soldiers buried in the city; the restoration of the Roger Williams Spring monument; the location of a permanent home for the East Providence Historical Society; the co-sponsorship, along with the Irish Ethnic Heritage Committee of Rhode Island, of a play in the high school auditorium; the identification of historic sites in the city in conjunction with the Rhode Island Preservation Commission in co-sponsorship with the

Members of the East Providence Bicentennial Committee honor winners of the 1st Bicentennial essay contest.

East Providence was chosen as a "National Bicentennial Community," and was awarded this flag in recognition of "superior Bicentennial planning and programs." At the City Hall presentation were, l. to r., Miss Gladys Wyatt of the Rhode Island Bicentennial Commission; Dr. Patrick T. Conley, Chairman and Director of the Rhode Island Bicentennial Commission; George Lamb, Mayor of East Providence; and Walter R. Martin, Chairman of the East Providence Bicentennial Committee.

Rumford Junior Women's Club city-wide "olympics"; support of the Young People's Theatre production; Heritage Days in both 1975 and 1976; and finally the publication of this comprehensive history of the city.

For these and other accomplished and contemplated activities, East Providence was chosen as a "National Bicentennial Community." A flag and certificate of recognition "of superior Bicentennial planning and programs" were presented to Mayor George A. Lamb and Committee Chairman Martin on August 18, 1975 by the regional director of the American Revolution Bicentennial Administration.

Perhaps the most important project launched by the Bicentennial Committee is the publication of this detailed history of East Providence. The people of the city will now have a clearer picture of the evolution of their community which should place them in a better position to face the future. This book expresses the Bicentennial Committee's conviction that an emotional or simply patriotic reaffirmation of our revolutionary tradition will not help us to solve modern problems or to see novel adaptations of that tradition. Understanding must go hand in hand with reaffirmation. With this in mind, let us distill the es-

East Providence officials "review the troops" as the Carpenter Militia visited City Hall in April, 1975.

The Rumford women march in the Heritage Day parade in April, 1975.

sence of the revolutionary tradition from East Providence's history.

In the first place, when we refer to a revolutionary tradition we are not speaking merely about the American Revolution, a handful of national heroes (Washington, Jefferson, Adams, etc.), or two sacred scrolls – the Declaration of Independence and the Constitution. American history was revolutionary from the beginning, and the events before, during and after 1776 were primarily applications and extensions – politicizations to be exact – of ideals that were present from the founding of America.

The early English settlers believed that they were establishing a "New Jerusalem." America was to be the "chosen land" where the Kingdom of God would become a reality. Here righteousness, harmony, peace, cooperation and justice would prevail in place of the corruption, discord and poverty of the Old World.

Such were the ideals that the Puritan and Pilgrim settlers espoused when they first came to America and which were reaffirmed whenever a new township was formed. (Recall the covenant which the people of

Old Rehoboth agreed to after settling the town.) The Revolution reasserted and secularized much of the religious idealism of early America and added the somewhat new dimension of political liberty. In the nineteenth and early twentieth centuries, large numbers of immigrants brought a new transfusion of hope to America's revolutionary tradition. By this time, under the pressure of industrialization, prosperity was fully recognized as an integral part of the promise of America.

This, then, is the revolutionary tradition. America offered a unique historical opportunity for people to live in peace and harmony with the prospect of economic success, and assured of political freedom. These are the ideals, but what about actuality? Here the history of East Providence "fleshens out" the promise of America, and provides a case study to test theory against reality.

What that history reveals is that many of America's ideals have become a reality. East Providence has been a prosperous, ever-expanding community, providing opportunities for its residents throughout its history. As a result of a major political reform movement in the twentieth century, which was certainly in the tradition of the American Revolution, an efficient, modern government was brought to the city.

Residents gathered for the dedication of the Fort Hill Monument in May of 1975.

But what the history of East Providence also reveals is that, because our nation was founded on such lofty theories, our history has never fully cohered with our cherished values. That is, America is a great nation, perhaps the greatest in the history of the world, but it is not so great that it has not at times fallen short of its professed ideals.

The history of East Providence demonstrates this clearly. Soon after the settlers of the East Providence area signed a cooperative covenant, for example, religious quarrels and political contention set neighbor against neighbor. A generation later, the self-doubt and gloom which accompanied King Philip's War were viewed by the inhabitants of Old Rehoboth as a punishment for not having lived up to their ideals. A similar interpretation was given to the Revolution, and this time the role of Providential chastiser was assumed not by Indians but by the British.

Next, a successful war for political liberty against Great Britain did not mean that the ideals of the Declaration of Independence would automatically become a reality. Instead, Old Rehoboth and nearly all of Massachusetts became embroiled in the sometimes violent uprising known as Shays' Rebellion. Then, two decades after the close of the Revolutionary era, Old Rehoboth was separated into two towns. This act was in defiance of the popular will, which the struggle against Great Britain had enshrined as the ultimate political arbiter.

What all this means is that there are points in the history of East Providence, in the history of America in general, where gaps appear between the revolutionary tradition and reality. It is hoped, then, that the Bicentennial celebration and particularly this book will help the people of the city to rededicate themselves to the ideals upon which our nation was founded, and upon which our future depends.

Appendix A

East Providence Territorial Changes, 1636-1862

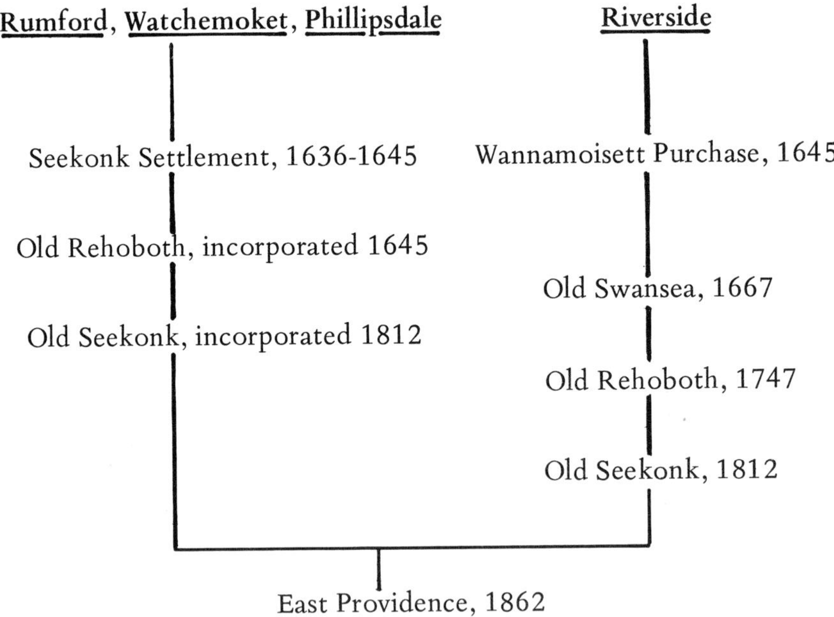

Appendix B

East Providence Population Chart

Year	Population
1865	2,172
1870	2,668
1875	4,336
1880	6,816
1890	8,422
1895	10,170
1900	12,138
1905	13,750
1910	15,808
1915	18,584
1920	21,793
1925	26,088
1930	29,995
1936	30,113
1940	32,165
1950	35,871
1960	41,955
1970	48,207

Selected Bibliography

Unpublished material:

American Electrical Works "Scrapbook," Washburn Wire Company, East Providence.

Canedy, Frank. "History of Narragansett Terrace," Typescript, East Providence, 1928.

Da Mota, Virginia. "The Portuguese of East Providence." Rhode Island College Ethnic Heritage Project, 1975.

East Providence City Records, 1862-1975, City Hall.

East Providence Council Records, 1862-1975, City Hall.

East Providence Land Records, 1696-1862, City Hall, Taunton, Massachusetts.

East Providence Land Records, 1862-1975, City Hall, East Providence.

"East Providence Refinery, 1920-1970." Typescript, East Providence, 1970.

East Providence School Committee Annual Reports, 1863-1919. School Department.

Erhardt, John. "First Exploreers in the Area of Old Seacunk," Typescript, Seekonk, 1968.

Ferst, Susan. "The Development of the Portuguese Community in Fox Point." Master's thesis, Brown University, 1972.

Flint, Harold. "A Territorial History of East Providence." Typescript, East Providence, n.d.

________. "History of Riverside." Typescript, East Providence, n.d.

________. "John Brown of Wannamoisett." Typescript, East Providence, n.d.

________. "Fort Hill." Typescript, East Providence, 1975.

Griswold, Arthur. "Fifty Years of the Fire Department in the Town of East Providence." Typescript, Central Fire Station, East Providence.

"Historical Papers Relating to the Town's History Commissioned by the League of Women Voters." Typescripts, Weaver Memorial Library, 1948.

"History of the East Providence Police Department." Typescript, East Providence, n.d.

"History of the Washburn Wire Company." Typescript, Washburn Wire Company. n.d.

Kumekawa, Glenn. "The American Negro Population of East Providence: An Analysis of the Migration Pattern to a Suburban Area." Master's thesis, Brown University, 1955.

Major, Helen. "A Historical Study of Public Education in East Providence, Rhode Island." Master's thesis, Rhode Island College, 1952.

Owen, William C. "Privateering and Piracy in Rhode Island, 1653-1712." Master's thesis, Brown University, 1959.

Rehoboth Town Records, 1645-1812. City Hall, Taunton, Massachusetts.

Rehoboth Proprietors Records. City Hall, Taunton, Massachusetts.

Reid, Owen. "History of St. Margaret's Church," Typescript, East Providence, n.d.

Rhode Island State Census Returns, "East Providence." 1905, 1915, 1925, 1935, State Records Center, Providence.

Rumford Chemical Works, "Records," Essex Chemical Company, East Providence.

Seekonk Town Records, 1813-1862. Seekonk Town Hall.

Sellew, Clinton. "Gravestone Records of Revolutionary War Patriots buried in East Providence, Rhode Island." East Providence, 1969.

Waddington, Alice. "A History of East Providence High School." Typescript, East Providence, 1952.

Walsh, Stephen. "All-America City Presentation of East Providence to the National Municipal League, November 1960." Typescript, East Providence, 1960.

Washburn Wire Company, "Records, 1901-1928," Washburn Wire Company, East Providence.

Wilson, Joe Harvey. "Soldier Relief Work in Rhode Island During the Civil War." Master's thesis, Brown University, 1931.

Newspapers:

The East Providence News

The East Providence Post

The Providence Journal

Published material:

Arnold, Samuel Greene. *History of the State of Rhode Island and Providence Plantations.* 2 vols., New York, 1859-60.

Baker, Virginia. *Sowams: The Home of Massasoit, Where Was It?* Boston, 1899.

Bates, Frank Greene. *Rhode Island and the Formation of the Union.* New York, 1967.

Bayles, Richard (ed.). *History of Providence County, Rhode Island.* 2 vols., New York, 1891.

Bicknell, Thomas. *The History of the State of Rhode Island and Providence Plantations.* 5 vols., New York, 1920.

———. *Historical Address, Poem, and Other Exercises at the Celebration of the Two Hundred and Fiftieth Anniversary of Rehoboth, Mass.* n.d., n.p.

Bliss, George. *An Historical Sketch of the Town of East Providence.* Providence, 1876.

Bliss, Leonard, Jr. *History of Rehoboth.* Boston, 1836.

Bodge, George. *Soldiers in King Philip's War.* Leominster, Mass. 1896.

Bowen, Richard Le Baron. *Early Rehoboth.* 4 vols., Rehoboth, 1946.

Caroll, Charles. *Rhode Island: Three Centuries of Democracy.* 4 vols., New York, 1932.

Chapin, A.A. *A History of Rhode Island Ferries, 1640-1923.* Providence, 1925.

Charter of the City of East Providence. East Providence, 1954.

Church, Benjamin and Thomas. *Entertaining History of King Philip's War.* Boston, 1716.

Coleman, Peter. *The Transformation of Rhode Island, 1790-1860.* Providence, 1963.

Dedication Exercises, Bridgham Memorial Library Building. Providence, 1905.

Demos, John. *A Little Commonwealth: Family Life in Plymouth Colony.* New York, 1970.

East Providence Planning Department Reports. 14 vols., East Providence, 1963-74.

East Providence Public School Manual. Providence, 1894.

East Providence Sewerage System Report. Providence, 1908.

Eighty Years of Baking Powder History. East Providence, 1908.

Emma Pendleton Bradley Home, Achievements of the First Ten Years, 1931-1941. Boston, 1941.

Federal Writers Project. *Rhode Island: A Guide to the Smallest State.* Boston, 1937.

Field, Edward. *State of Rhode Island and Providence Plantations at the End of the Century.* 3 vols., Boston, 1902.

Gleason, Paul. *Rhode Island: The Development of a Democracy.* Providence, 1957.

Greene, Albert. *Historical Address. . .in Commemoration of the 100th Anniversary of the Founding of the First Baptist Church in East Providence, Rhode Island.* Providence, 1894.

Handbook of Historical Sites in Rhode Island. Providence, 1936.

Historical Address and Poem Delivered in the Newman Congregational Church, June 7, 1893, in Commemoration of the 250th Anniversary of the Founding of the Newman Congregational Church and Ancient Town of Rehoboth. Pawtucket, 1893.

Historical Sketch of the First Baptist Church of East Providence, n.d., n.p.

History of the Providence and Worcester Railroad Company. Boston, 1966.

Howe, George. *Mount Hope: A New England Chronicle.* New York, 1959.

Hoyt, Harold. *The Story of Hunt's Mills.* Providence, 1895.

Hurricane 1938. Providence, 1938.

Hutchinson, John. *Rhode Island Boundaries, 1636-1936.* Providence, 1936.

Kimball, Gertrude. *Pictures of Rhode Island in the Past, 1642-1833, by Travellers and Observers.* Providence, 1900.

Leach, Douglas. *Flintlock and Tomahawk: New England in King Philip's War.* New York, 1958.

Lockridge, Kenneth. *A New England Town: The First Hundred Years.* New York, 1970.

Lovejoy, David. *Rhode Island in the Revolution.* Providence, 1960.

Manual of the Newman Congregational Church. Providence, 1902.

Miller, Perry. *Roger Williams: His Contribution to the American Tradition.* New York, 1962.

Mohr, Ralph. *Governors of Three Hundred Years, 1638-1954, Rhode Island and Providence Plantations.* Providence, 1954.

Morgan, Edmund. *Roger Williams on Church and State.* New Haven, 1963.

Munro, Wilfred. *Picturesque Rhode Island.* Providence, 1881.

Newman, Sylvanus Chase. *Rehoboth in the Past.* Pawtucket, 1860.

Order of Service Appointed for laying the Corner Stone of the East Providence Town Hall. Providence, 1888.

Polk's East Providence Directory. Boston, 1950.

Prospectus of the Riverside Land Company, n.d., n.p.

Report Concerning the Erection of a Bridge across the Seekonk River at the Site of Central Bridge. Providence, 1869.

Report of a Committee to Investigate the Various Sources of Water Supply Available for Furnishing Water to the East Providence Fire District. Providence, 1892.

Rhode Island Civil War Chronicles, No. 1. Providence, 1960.

Rhode Island State Census Reports, 1865, 1875, 1885, 1895. Providence, 1865-1895.

Richman, Irving. *Rhode Island: Its Making and Meaning.* New York, 1902.

Rider, Sidney. *A Retrospect from the Round Tower of the Pomham Club.* Providence, 1889.

Rutman, Darrett. *Husbandmen of Plymouth: Farms and Villages in the Old Colony, 1620-1692.* Boston, 1967.

Shurtleff, Nathaniel and Pulsifer, David (eds.). *Records of the Colony of New Plymouth, in New England.* Boston, 1855-61.

Smith, Otho. "History of East Providence" in *REP Art Exhibit.* Providence, 1969.

Squantum Association. Providence, 1902.

Stone, Edwin. *Rhode Island in the Rebellion.* Providence, 1864.

Sylvester, Herbert. *Indian Wars of New England.* 3 vols., Boston, 1910.

Tilton, George. *A History of Rehoboth.* Boston, 1916.

*   *   *

It is the hope of the East Providence Bicentennial Committee that this history, and participation in the activities commemorating our Bicentennial, will move all the citizens of East Providence and beyond to a greater sense of community and purpose. When East Providence joins in the celebration of the nation's tercentenary, may it be said that the intervening 100 years brought our city and country closer to fulfilling the "promise of American life."